Albanian Poetry

An Elusive Eagle Soars

Edited and translated
with an introduction by
Robert Elsie

FOREST
BOOKS
London & Boston

UNESCO

UNESCO COLLECTION OF REPRESENTATIVE WORKS
European series

This book has been accepted in the translations
collection of the United Nations Educational Scientific
and Cultural Organisation (UNESCO)

PUBLISHED BY
FOREST BOOKS
20 Forest View, Chingford, London E4 7AY, UK
PO Box 312, Lincoln Centre, MA 01773, USA

FIRST PUBLISHED
1993

Typeset in Great Britain by Cover to Cover, Cambridge
Printed in Great Britain by BPCC Wheatons Ltd, Exeter

The publication of this work has been authorised by the
Albanian National Commission for UNESCO.

A CIP catalogue record for this book is
available from the British Library

ISBN 1 85610 017 0

Library of Congress Catalog Card No: 92-75076

Contents

Contents

iv

Contents

Contents

Introduction

Two hundred years ago, Edward Gibbon described Albania as a land within sight of Italy and less known than the interior of America. The spirit of this quotation has lost surprisingly little of its validity over the last two centuries. Albania, bordering on Greece and what has been Yugoslavia, and less than one hundred kilometres from the southern Italian coast, has, until very recently, been no better known to most Europeans than Tibet or Timbuktu.

The Albanians are probably among the oldest inhabitants of southeastern Europe, claiming descent from the ancient Illyrians, although due to the lack of linguistic records the exact strength of the Illyrian element in Albania is difficult to determine. Fathoming the genesis of a people is particularly difficult in the Balkan peninsula, which has baffled scholars from Herodotus to recent generations of history students trying to sort out the Balkan wars.

The Albanian language

The Albanian language, now spoken by about six million people in the Balkans, is divided into two basic dialect groups: Geg (or Gheg) in the north and Tosk in the south. The Shkumbin river in central Albania, flowing past Elbasan into the Adriatic, forms the approximate border between the two dialect groups. The Geg dialect group is characterized by the presence of nasal vowels, by the retention of the older *n* for Tosk *r* (e.g. *venë* 'wine' for Tosk *verë*, *Shqypnia* 'Albania' for Tosk *Shqipëria*) and by several distinct morphological features. The modern literary language (*gjuha letrare*), agreed upon, though not without political pressure, in 1972, is a combination of the two dialect groups, but based to about 80% on Tosk. It is now a widely accepted standard both in Albania, Kosovo and Macedonia.

In addition to three million speakers in Albania itself, the Albanian language is also spoken by two to three million individuals in what was once Yugoslavia, where it is second only to Serbo-Croatian. The Albanian population is to be found primarily in Kosovo (Alb. *Kosova*) with its capital Prishtinë. With the disintegration of Yugoslavia, the people of the once autonomous region proclaimed the Republic of Kosovo, though they are still de facto under harsh Serbian political and military control. In Kosovo, the Albanians now make up about 90% of the population, the other 10% being primarily Serbian and Turkish speakers. The three languages were until recently all officially recognized and in full use in every sphere of life in the politically and economically troubled region. The mother tongue of most Kosovo Albanians is the northeastern Geg dialect referred to above, though virtually all publications here, as in Albania, are now in standard literary Albanian. Radio and television broadcasting and schooling from kindergarten to university also took place in standard literary Albanian until the Serbian military takeover put an end to them. The Albanians have an extremely high birth-rate and their proportion of the population in Kosovo and in Macedonia is increasing year by year. The southern Republic of Macedonia has an Albanian-speaking minority of at least a quarter of the total population. Skopje (Alb. *Shkup*), which, much to the distress of the Macedonians, is ironically said to have the largest Albanian population of any city on earth, serves as a secondary centre for Albanian publishing and culture, though it is far less important than Prishtinë itself, which can now vie with Tiranë in every way as a focal point of Albanian literary and cultural activity and as a publishing centre for Albanian literature. A substantial minority of Albanian speakers (about 10%) is also to be found in Montenegro, mostly along the Albanian border, e.g. in the regions of Guci and Plavë in the mountains, Tuz south of Podgorica (Titograd) and Ulcinj on the southern Yugoslav coast. There are, in addition, Albanian speakers throughout southern Serbia and indeed in virtually all other regions of the disintegrating Yugoslav federation, many of whom have fled from the economically destitute Kosovo region to the more affluent northern republics (Croatia and Slovenia) in search of freedom, jobs and a better standard of living. Numerous Kosovo Albanians are also to be found among the migrant workers of western Europe, in particular in Switzerland and in Germany.

A surprise to many is the existence of an Albanian minority in southern Italy, the so-called *Arbëresh*. These are the descendants of refugees who fled Albania after the death of Scanderbeg in 1468. Due to a more favourable social and political environment than that existing in the Balkans, the Arbëresh were able to make a decisive contribution to the evolution of Albanian literature and to the nationalist movement in the nineteenth century. Older Albanian literature is indeed to a large extent Arbëresh literature. As a linguistic minority, the Arbëresh now consist of about 90,000 speakers, most of whom live in the mountain villages of Cosenza in Calabria and in the vicinity of Palermo in Sicily. Their language, which still does not benefit from the official status accorded to other national minorities in Italy (German, French, Slovenian etc.), is moribund due to the strong cultural influence of Italian and to economic emigration. It is extremely archaic and differs substantially from the Albanian now spoken in the Balkans such that communication is difficult if Arbëresh speakers are not familiar with standard literary Albanian.

In Greece, the sizeable stratum of Albanians who populated much of central and southern Greece in the Middle Ages has been largely assimilated. The Albanian language there, known in Greek as *Arvanitika*, can nonetheless still be heard in about 320 villages, primarily those of Boeotia (especially around Levadhia), southern Euboea, Attica, Corinth and the Peloponnese, and northern Andros. No official statistics exist as to the number of speakers since the language does not enjoy any official status. *Arvanitika*, which is dying out rapidly, is thought to be the most archaic form of Albanian spoken today.

A large Albanian community still exists in Turkey (Istanbul and elsewhere). The ranks of these Turkish Albanians were swelled by an estimated 230,000 Yugoslav Albanians who were unjustly expelled from their native land between 1953 and 1966 and forced to emigrate to Turkey.

Finally, Albanian speakers in varying numbers are to be encountered in countries of immigration such as the United States (Boston, New York, Detroit), Australia, Canada and Argentina.

Introduction

Albanian literature

Compared to the other national languages of Europe, Albanian does not enjoy a long literary tradition. In fact, it was the last national language of Europe to be recorded. Nor has the establishment of a literary culture in Albania ever been an easy task, though not for want of artistic endeavour and creative impulses. All too often the tempestuous course of Albanian history has nipped the flowers of Albanian literature in the bud and severed the roots of intellectual culture.

Sixteenth and seventeenth century Albanian literature, with its primarily religious focus (biblical translations and devotional texts), beginning with the 'Missal' of Gjon Buzuku in 1555, might have provided a foundation for literary creativity in the age of the Counter-Reformation under the somewhat ambiguous patronage of the Catholic church, had not the banners of Islam soon been unfurled on the eastern horizons, and tiny Albania been destined to bear the full brunt of the Turkish invasion. The Ottoman colonization of Albania, which had begun as early as 1385, was to split the country into three spheres of culture, all virtually independent of one another: (1) the cosmopolitan traditions of the Islamic Orient using initially Turkish, Persian and Arabic as their media of literary expression and later Albanian in a stylized Aljamiado literature, the so-called poetry of the *Bejtexhinj*; (2) the lingering Byzantine heritage of Greek Orthodoxy in southern Albania which produced a number of religious and scholarly works in Greek script in the 18th century; and (3) the awakening culture and literature of the *Arbëresh* (Italo-Albanians) in southern Italy, nourished by a more favourable social, political and economic climate and by the fertile intellectual soil of Italian civilization.

The stable foundations of an Albanian national literature were finally laid in the second half of the nineteenth century with the rise of the nationalist movement striving for independence from a decaying Ottoman Empire. The literature of this so-called *Rilindja* period of national awakening was one of romantic nationalism and provides an excellent key to an understanding of the Albanian mentality even today. As so often in the history of Albanian literature, writing in Albanian, by its very existence, constituted an act of defiance against the foreign powers ruling the country or dominating it culturally. Indeed, the Sublime Porte rightly regarded most Albanian cultural and educational activity as subversive, and as such, saw fit to ban Albanian-language schools and the publication of all books and periodicals in Albanian. With no access to education in their own language, only a small minority of Albanians could hope to break through the barriers to intellectual thought and literary creativity.

At the beginning of the twentieth century, the Catholic education facilities set up by the Jesuits and Franciscans in Shkodër (Scutar) under the auspices of the *Kultusprotektorat* paved the way for the creation of an intellectual elite in Albania which in turn produced the rudiments of a more sophisticated literature that expressed itself primarily in verse. The culmination of Albanian literature before the Second World War can be seen in the works of the talented Franciscan pater Gjergj Fishta (1871–1940), once lauded as the national poet of Albania, and for reasons more political than literary, later ostracized from the Albanian Parnassus.

The flourishing literature of pre-war Albania was swept away by the political revolution which took place in the country during and after the Second World War, to be replaced by a radically proletarian and socialist literature in its infancy. This literature was to remain in its infancy, however, since the terror exerted upon writers and intellectuals by the Stalinist regime which came to power in 1944 created a cultural vacuum that lasted for over two decades. The results of this period of fear and stagnation can still be felt today.

With the coming to power of the communists led by Enver Hoxha (1908–1985), substantial efforts were nonetheless made for the first time to provide the broad masses of the population with basic education. The post-war mass literacy campaign which was concluded fairly recently, constituted a revolution in itself, and paved the way for a real national literature that could encompass all strata of society. In order to appreciate the reasons for the comparatively late blossoming of a written literature in Albania, one must keep in mind the fact that up to the not so distant 1950s, eighty percent of the population of the country, including virtually all the women, were in fact illiterate. The twentieth century arrived late in Albania.

Poetry has always been the *élan vital* of Albanian literature; original prose is a newer genre and professional theatre, the

xiii

prerogative of an urban society, was virtually unknown in Albania until recent times. The earliest recorded poem in Albanian, written by the Sicilian cleric Luca Matranga (Alb. *Lekë Matrënga*), dates from 1592. With the exception of Pjetër Budi (1566–1622), an interest in verse among other early Christian authors remained sporadic. The Moslem culture of seventeenth and eighteenth century Albania, however, produced a substantial amount of oriental verse in Albanian, written in Arabic script, the poetry of the *Bejtexhinj*, much of which remains to be discovered. The romantic nationalism characteristic of verse of the *Rilindja* period of the late nineteenth century, when Albania was struggling for its independence, lasted well into the first decades of the twentieth century.

Modern Albanian poetry can be said to date from the 1930s. It begins its course with two poets in particular: Migjeni (1911–1938) and Lasgush Poradeci (1899–1987). Migjeni (acronym of Millosh Gjergj Nikolla) from Shkodër, who died of tuberculosis at the tender age of twenty-six, was one of the first poets to abandon the long-standing tradition of romantic nationalism in Albanian verse. His poetry, collected in the slender volume 'Free Verse', is characterized by a strong social ethic, not of pity for the poor, but of outrage against injustice and oppression. Lasgush Poradeci from the town of Pogradec on Lake Ohrid, on the other hand, who had very little in common with his contemporaries – the romantic Asdreni (1872–1947), the political Fan Noli (1882–1965) or the messianic Migjeni – imbued Albanian letters with an exotic element of pantheistic mysticism, introducing what he called the metaphysics of creative harmony. An eclectic child of his age, Poradeci was and remains one of the many paradoxes of southeastern European literature. Kosovo critic Rexhep Qosja notes aptly that he felt like a Romantic, thought like a Classic, was as solitary and spiritually hermetic as a Symbolist and as formally precise as a Parnassist. Although he remained an outsider, his stylistic finesse was decisive in enriching and diversifying Albanian poetic metres.

Literature of the fifties and early sixties saw the pervasion in Albania of the doctrine of socialist realism which encouraged a definite social and political message, not only in prose but also in verse. The link between literature and Marxist politics was firmly cemented. In a preface to *Anthologie de la poésie albanaise* (Tiranë 1983), conservative critic Dalan Shapllo defined the mission of poetry in socialist realism as 'serving the masses, giving them spiritual sustenance and emotional satisfaction'. It was a mission destined from the very start to failure. All writers in Albania came under the 'critical guidance' of the Party of Labour, a surveillance more attune to a socialist surrealism. Prose writers were 'encouraged' to concentrate their creative energies on specific themes such as the partisan struggle of the 'national liberation war' and on the building of socialism. Subjects devoid of any redeeming educational value in Marxist terms were considered alien and taboo. Socialist realism gave writers the tools with which to create but, as an absolute value, it allowed them no alternatives.

A turning point came in the stormy year of 1961 which, on the one hand, marked the dramatic political break with the Soviet Union and thus with Soviet literary models, and on the other hand witnessed the publication of a number of trend-setting volumes of verse: *Shekulli im* (My century) by Ismail Kadare (1936—), *Hapat e mija në asfalt* (My steps on the pavement) by Dritëro Agolli (1931—), and in the following year *Shtigje poetike* (Poetic paths) by Fatos Arapi (1930—). The attempt made by this generation of intellectuals educated in the eastern bloc to exploit the break with the Soviet Union in order to broaden the literary horizon led to a vigorous literary controversy at a meeting of the Albanian Union of Writers and Artists in Tiranë on 11 July 1961. It pitted writers of the older generation such as Andrea Varfi (1914—), Luan Qafëzezi (1922—) and Mark Gurakuqi (1922–1977), who voiced their support for fixed poetic standards and the solid traditions of Albanian literature and who opposed new elements such as free verse as un-Albanian, against a new generation led by Ismail Kadare, Dritëro Agolli, Fatos Arapi and Dhori Qiriazi (1933—) who favoured a literary renewal and a broadening of the stylistic and thematic horizon. The road to renewal was given the green light by Enver Hoxha himself who saw that the situation was untenable.

Though it constituted no radical change of course, no liberalization or political 'thaw' in the Soviet sense, 1961 set the stage for a quarter of a century of trial and error, which led to much greater sophistication in Albanian literature. Despite the terror waged against intellectuals during Enver Hoxha's 1973 campaign against liberalism and foreign influences, themes and styles did diversify and more attention was gradually paid to formal literary criteria and to the question of individuality. Fortunately, the assigned mission of the poet was soon combined with enough creativity and talent to save contemporary Albanian lyrics from the sterile panegyrics which party dogmatists usually long for.

The Albanian literature of Kosovo was late to develop. The extreme political divergence between Yugoslavia and Albania which erupted in 1948 made it evident to Kosovo Albanians from the start that they could not look to Tiranë for more than moral support in culture and education. The preservation and fostering of Albanian culture in Yugoslavia under often hostile conditions was of necessity to be the concern of Yugoslav Albanians themselves. The formidable problems posed by widespread illiteracy and dire poverty among the Albanians in Kosovo, as in Albania, were compounded substantially by an unwillingness on the part of the Serbian authorities in Belgrade for many years to give the Albanians access to education and cultural facilities in their own language. Full cultural autonomy was first achieved after much delay under the constitution of 1974, though only in Kosovo itself. In 1989/1990, however, Kosovo de facto lost its limited autonomy and freedom and was placed under direct Serbian military occupation. Immediately after the dissolution of the Kosovo parliament in the summer of 1990, the only Albanian-language daily newspaper was banned as was all Albanian radio and television broadcasting in Kosovo. In the autumn of 1991 teaching at the University of Prishtinë was suspended with the exception of classes reserved for the small Serbian minority. The situation has been particularly dire for Albanian writers and intellectuals there.

Nonetheless, the rapidly developing literature of the Kosovo Albanians, though lacking the rich literary traditions of Slovenian, Serbian and Croatian, can now easily keep pace. By the next century, the Albanian language will no doubt be the second most important vehicle of literary expression in what was once the Yugoslav federation. The modern literature of Kosovo is just as dynamic as that of

Albania proper and, with regard to the diversity and expressiveness of its poetry, often surpasses that of the motherland. Without the ideological constraints which were imposed on literature and culture in Tiranë, the literature of Kosovo was able to flourish relatively free of dogma. It is thus more experimental and offers the reader a wider range of styles, subject matter and ideas.

Is there a poet slumbering in every Albanian? Publishing statistics would certainly indicate a strong preference for verse over prose. In Tiranë about 40% of literary publications over the past few years have been poetry, and in Prishtinë up to 70%, something quite unimaginable in the rational West.

Albanian literature is a young and dynamic literature reflecting a culture quite unique in Europe. But perhaps no European literature has been so neglected by Western readers, a neglect fostered by the lack of available translations, the lack of specialists in Albanian, and over the last half a century by Albania's political isolation. If Edward Gibbon's remark about Albania is still valid, the real *terra incognita* is Albanian literature.

The present anthology is but a first step to introduce Albanian literature to the English-speaking reader. By including selections from the best known poets of Albania, of the Albanian population of Kosovo and Macedonia and of the diaspora, it endeavours to be representative of modern Albanian verse production as a whole, though it is obvious that many more volumes would be needed to provide comprehensive coverage of all modern Albanian literature.

In conclusion, I should like to thank all those who have helped and encouraged me in this project, including my friends and colleagues of the Albanian Writers' Union (Tiranë), the University of Prishtinë, the Albanological Institute (Prishtinë) and the Writers' Union of Kosovo (Prishtinë). Particular thanks also go to Barbara Schultz (Ottawa) for her excellent assistance with the manuscript.

Robert Elsie
Olzheim/Eifel, Germany
Spring 1992

Linguist, translator and critic, Robert Elsie was born in Vancouver, Canada, in 1950. He studied at the University of British Columbia, the Free University of Berlin, the Ecole Pratique des Hautes Etudes in Paris and the Dublin Institute for Advanced Studies, finishing his doctorate in Celtic Studies at the University of Bonn in 1978. In addition to numerous translations, he is the author of *Dictionary of Albanian Literature* (New York, 1986) and *Dialect Relationships in Goidelic* (Hamburg, 1986).

A note on Albanian Pronunciation

Letter	Pronunciation
c	as in Eng. bits
ç	as in Eng. child
dh	as in Eng. this
ë	neutral schwa vowel, as in Eng. about, Germ. bitte
gj	voiced palatal plosive, as in Croatian đak, Hungarian Magyar
j	as in Eng. yes
l	palatal l. as in Ital. voglio
ll	velar l. as in Eng. table
nj	palatal n. as in Fr. cognac, Span. pequeño
q	voiceless palatal plosive, as in Croatian treći
r	simple flapped r. as in Span. pero
rr	rolled r. as in Span. perro. Scottish Edinburgh
sh	as in Eng. she
th	as in Eng. thing
x	as in Eng. foods
xh	as in Eng. jam
y	rounded high vowel, as in Fr. tu, Germ. grün
zh	as in Eng. measure, Brezhnev

Note that place names can be written with or without the postpositive definite article, e.g.: Elbasani, Elbasan; Durresi, Durrës; Tirana, Tiranë; Shkodra, Shkodër.

xix

Approximate Extent
of Current Albanian Settlement

xx

Lasgush Poradeci

(1899–1987)

At the end of 1987 the last great classic writer of twentieth-century Albanian verse, Lazar Gusho, who wrote under the pseudonym Lasgush Poradeci, died at the age of eighty-seven. He had spent the final years of his life in his beloved town of Pogradec on Lake Ohrid, not far from the border of the former Yugoslavia, tending his garden à la Candide and studying the ever-changing moods of the lake. The gentle and rhythmic lapping of the waves had always been among the fundamental sources of his pantheistic verse.

Poradeci was born in Pogradec in 1899, being but a few days older than the twentieth century, as he once remarked. He attended a Romanian-language school in Monastir (Bitola), Macedonia, a French Catholic lycée in Athens and the Academy of Fine Arts in Bucharest, where a sizeable colony of Albanian exiles had grown up. His stay in Bucharest was to have a decisive influence on his literary development. It was there that he met and befriended the Albanian romantic poet Asdreni (1872–1947), and began publishing verse in various Albanian-language periodicals (*Shqipëri e Re* of Constanza and *Dielli* of Boston among others), revealing a certain theosophical affinity to the Romanian lyric poet Mihai Eminescu. A scholarship provided by the Fan Noli government in 1924 enabled him to continue his studies of Romance and Germanic philology in Graz, Austria, where he spent the happiest years of his life. From 1934 to the end of the war, he taught secondary school in Tiranë and thereafter worked as a translator for the state-owned Naim Frashëri Publishing Company until retirement. His two major collections of poetry, *Vallja e yjve* (The dance of the stars) and *Ylli i zemrës* (The star of the heart), were published in Romania in 1933 and 1937 respectively.

Pogradec

A shimmering sunset on the endless lake.
Ghostlike, a veil is slowly spread.
Over mountain and meadow the dark of night descends,
Settling from the heavens upon the town.

Over the vast land no more sound is to be heard:
In the village the creaking of a door,
On the lake the silence of an oar.
Over the Mal i Thatë an elusive eagle soars.
My youthful heart retreats into the depths of my soul.

The whole town, all life, retires to the realm of sleep.
Darkness rules the four quarters of the earth. And now,
Setting out on his journey through Albania,
Legendary Father Drin arises at St. Naum's.*

---

* The poet's beloved Pogradec is a little town on the Albanian side of Lake
Ohrid in which the river Drin takes its source. Not far from Pogradec, now
just across the border on the Macedonian side, is the famous mediaeval
church of St. Naum's overlooking the lake. Behind the church rises the Mal
i Thatë (Dry Mountain) which separates Lake Ohrid from Lake Prespa.

Morning

Like a spirit sombre within the breast
Lies the lake encased in hills.
Mirrored in its depths,
Night expires breath by breath.

I watch how she suffers, how she dies,
Her eyes blinking,
Azure-circled pools,
Like the stars of a fading sky.

But now the light of dawn
Shimmers deep within the lake.
The daystar steals away, melting
Like a piece of sugar candy.

Behold, day has dawned,
And lightning flashes from the depths.
Like a harbinger of morn
Appears, bird-white, a pelican.

End of autumn

The last stork flew off, majestic and forlorn,
Soaring over the snowy mountains at the break of day,
After tapping on the door with his sturdy beak,
Leaving his nest to the master's care and departing heavy
                                                    of heart.

No longer does the fateful bird comb the ploughed fields,
The furrows cut into the soil by mountain oxen,
No longer is the grey mouse heard scurrying over fallow
                                                    land,
In the barren brake the speckled snake is dead.

Beneath the icy wind, the hoary earth lies silent,
The north wind howls through the withered trees.
As the cold grips harder, a clever little wren
Chatters blithely over hedge and over sedge.

Oh, how graceful was the stork, how slender and noble,
Pacing slowly like a bridegroom crowned!
At his side, with radiant breast, the crane,
With measured step, eyes uplifted – played his bride!

4

Winter

From today my spirit is a recluse,
And banished is all my joy.
Long has it been that snow has lain
Over mountain and over wood.

Snowflakes come drifting one by one
Down upon the deserted village
And, shivering beneath the snow,
Earth slumbers, buried once again.

Slowly my spirit too sinks to the ground
In mourning, falling like a leaf.
Nary a soul is to be heard,
No people, no sign of life.

In such peace and tranquillity
I hear a bird lament,
Letting out a faint sigh,
Frightened to leave this life.

Migjeni

(1911–1938)

With Migjeni (acronym of Millosh Gjergj Nikolla), contemporary Albanian poetry begins its course.

Born in Shkodër (Scutari) on 13 October 1911 of a family of Serbian origin, Migjeni studied as a child at the Serbian-language school there and later at St. John's Orthodox Seminary in Bitola (Manastir), Macedonia, where he became acquainted with Serbo-Croatian, Russian and French authors. On his return to Albania, he gave up his intended career as a priest to become a school teacher in Vrakë, a village a few miles from Shkodër, and began writing verse and prose sketches in Albanian. Having contracted tuberculosis, which was then endemic in Albania, he went for treatment to Turin in northern Italy where his sister Olga was studying at the university. After some time in a sanatorium there he was transferred to the Waldensian Hospital in Torre Pellice where he died on 26 August 1938 at the age of twenty-six.

His slender volume of verse (forty-three poems in all) entitled *Vargjet e lira* (Free verse) was published after much delay in Tiranë in 1944.

Preface of prefaces

Day by day the gods decline,
Their images slipping over
The years and centuries,
And now, no one knows who is god and who is man.
In the brain of mankind god is crouched,
Fingertips pressed to his temples
In sign of remorse
And in his bitter regret cries out:
What, oh what have I created?
Man does not know
Whether god is his creation
Or he a creation of god,
But he sees that it is folly
To meditate upon an idol
That answers not.
And now, no one knows who is god and who is man.
A time has come
When men understand one another well enough
To build the Tower of Babel –
And at the top of the Tower, to the highest throne
Man will mount
And thence cry out:
God! Where are you?

The sons of the new age

We, the sons of the new age,
Leaving the old to its 'holiness',
Have clenched our fists to fight
In new battles
And to triumph . . .
We, the sons of the new age,
Scions of a soil drenched in tears
Where the sweat of our brows has been shed in vain,
For our land was the prey of foreigners
Whose fury had to be paid for dearly . . .
We, the sons of the new age,
Brothers born and raised in misery,
When our ultimate and joyful hour
Rang out
We learned to say:
We will not be lost

In the bloody game of human history.
No! no! We will not be forever lost.
We shall have victory!
Victory of conscience and of free thought!
Nor will we,
For the sake of degenerates
Of the past in search of 'sanctity',
Wallow again into the mire of misery
And return once more to our sad lament,
Our monotonous lifeless lament of bondage,
And be but an irritation in the human brain.
We, the sons of the new age,
With our all-consuming ardour,
Will take up new battles
And sacrifice ourselves for victory.

Songs unsung

Deep within me sleep songs unsung,
Which neither suffering nor joy have yet brought forth,
Which sleep on awaiting a happier day
To burst out and be sung withour fear or grief.

Deep within me my songs are dormant . . .
I am a volcano, lying quiescent,
But when the day comes, they will all burst out,
In a thousand immortal colours spout.

But will the day come for my songs to awaken?
Or will the ages continue their derision?
No! no! Because freedom has begun to bloom
And I feel the warmth of the (allegoric) Sun.

Oh, sleeping songs, my personal relics,
Still to any other heart unknown.
Only I, like a child, with you am content,
I – your cradle, and perhaps your tomb.

Poem of poverty

Poverty, brothers, is something hard to swallow,
A mouthful that sticks in your throat and leaves you
in sorrow,
When you see the pale faces and rheumy eyes
Which watch you like ghosts and hold out thin hands;
And thus behind you stretched out they remain
Their whole lives through, until they die.
Above them in the air, as if in disdain,
Crosses and minarets of stone pierce the sky,
Prophets and saints of many colours arrayed
Radiate splendour. And poverty feels betrayed.

Poverty hides its own vile imprint;
It is hideous, evil, disgraceful.
The brow that bears it, the eyes that express it,
The lips that try in vain to hide it
Are the off-spring of ignorance, the victims of disdain,
The filthy scraps flung from the table,
On which for centuries
A ravenous insatiable dog has fed.
Poverty has no fortune, only rags,
The tattered banners of a hope,
Shattered by broken promises.

Poverty wallows in debauchery
In dark corners, together with dogs, rats, cats,
On mouldy, stinking, filthy mattresses
Naked breasts exposed, sallow dirty bodies,
Where feelings overwhelmed by bestial desire,
Bite, suck, devour, kiss the sullied lips,
And in unbridled lust the thirst is quenched,
The craving satisfied, and self-consciousness lost.
And that is the source of the imbeciles, the servants and
the beggars
Who will be born tomorrow to fill the streets.

Poverty shining in the eyes of the new-born
Flickers like the pale flame of the candle

11

Under a ceiling black with smoke and spider webs,
Where human shadows tremble on damp-stained walls,
Where the ailing infant wails like a banshee,
To suck the dry breasts of its wretched mother,
Who, pregnant again, curses god and the devil,
Curses the heavy burden of her unborn child.
Her baby does not laugh, but only cries,
Unwanted by its mother, who curses it, too.
How sorrowful is the cradle of the poor
Where a child is rocked with tears and sighs.

Poverty's child is raised in the shadows
Of great mansions, too high for imploring voice to reach,
To disturb the peace of gentlemen
Sleeping oblivious with their wives.

Poverty matures a child before its time,
Teaches it to dodge the threatening fist,
The hand which clutches its throat in dreams,
When the delirium of starvation sets in.
And death casts its shadow on childish faces.
Instead of a smile, a hideous grimace.
When the fate of a fruit is to ripen and fall,
– the child is interred without ripening at all.

Poverty labours and toils by night and day,
Chest and forehead drenched in sweat,
Smeared to the knees with sticky clay,
And still the empty guts contract from hunger.
Starvation wages! For grinding toil all day
Only three or four leks and an 'On your way'.

Poverty sometimes has a painted face,
Swollen lips scarlet, hollow cheeks rouged,
And body a chattel in a filthy trade,
For services in bed for which it is paid
With a few lousy francs,
Soiled sheets, soiled face and soiled conscience.

Poverty leaves a heritage as well
– not cash in the bank or property you can sell,

12

But distorted bones and pains in the chest.
Perhaps it leaves the memory of a bygone day
When the roof of the house, weakened by decay,
By age and the weather, collapsed and fell
And above all the din rose a terrible cry,
Cursing and imploring, as from the depths of hell,
The voice of a man crushed by a beam.
And so under the heel of God irate
Says the priest – ends the life of a dissolute ingrate.
And so the memory of such misfortunes
Fills the cup of bitterness inherited by generations.

Poverty in drink seeks consolation,
In filthy taverns, with dirty, littered tables
The thirsting soul pours liquor down his throat
In order to forget a thousand troubles,
The dulling glass, the glass satanic,
With its venemous bite gives comfort.
And when the man collapses to the floor
He giggles and sobs, a tragicomic clown.
All his sorrow in drink he drowns
And one by one a hundred glasses downs.

Poverty sets desires ablaze like stars in the night
And turns them to ashes, like tree trunks struck by lightning.

Poverty knows not joy, but only pain.
Unbearable pain which drives you crazy,
So you seize the rope and hang yourself,
Or become a poor victim of 'paragraphs'.

Poverty wants no pity, only justice!
Pity? Bastard daughter of cunning fathers,
Who like the Pharisees, beating the drum
Ostentiously for their own sly ends,
Drop a penny in the beggar's hand.

Poverty is an indelible stain
On the brow of humanity through the ages.
And this stain can never be effaced,
With the doctrines mouldering in temples.

Blasphemy

The mosques and churches float through our memories,
Prayers devoid of sense or taste echo from their walls.
Never has the heart of god yet been touched by them
But still beats on amidst the sounds of drums and bells.

Majestic mosques and churches throughout our wretched
land,
Spires and minarets towering over lowly homes,
The voice of hodja and of priest in one degenerate chant,
Oh, ideal vision, a thousand years old!

The mosques and churches float through memories of the
pious,
The sounds of the bell mingle with the muezzin's call,
Sanctity shines from cowls and the beards of hodjas.
Oh, so many beauteous angels at the gates of hell!

On their ancient citadels perch the carrion crows
Their wings drooping dejectedly – the symbols of lost hopes,
They croak despairingly about an age gone by
When their ancient citadels once gleamed with hallowed joy.

Broken melody

Broken melody – tear sparkling in the eye
Of a woman loved . . .
Pleasure past,
Jewel lost,
A trampled dream,
Lips unkissed
In the broken melody.

With silent sobs the naked shoulders shake,
Their whiteness dazzling . . .
Stabbed, stabbed with remorse
For the moments of mindlessness,
For her ruined fate,
For the happiness lost
In the broken melody.

Face hidden in her hands in shame,
Remorsefully the woman weeps,
With heart despairing
(a broken guitar,
A voice stifled
On lips kissed by pain
In the broken melody).

Silent he stands beside the woman weeping
Scolding tears of shame
That dim her eyes.
Some money on the table quickly lays
And goes away,
Leaving the woman lost
In the broken melody.

But when another comes, lust mounts again,
The heated blood
Pounds furiously through the veins,
Benumbing mind
. . . and only gasps
And grunts are heard
In the horrid melody.

Song of noble grief

Oh, noble grief of the suffering soul
That bursts out in the free verses . . .
Did you hope the world to console
And prettify life's reverses?

Oh, noble grief in the verses free,
Which sound and resound so sincere,
Will you move the feelings of men
Or wither and die forgotten?

Oh, song worthy of noble grief,
Cease not your lamentation,
Continue to sing about poverty,
For time will bring consolation.

The lost rhyme

Life to him was a glass of champagne.
Nights led him to the beds of women
Who loved him, but more for his money
Than for the nibble of his teeth.

And the curtain fell . . .
The protagonist died . . .

But the champagne lives on!

Millions are born
With billions of desires.
Whose turn will it be
When the idlers are gone?

But there will always be Carneras*
Always be the poet
As well as the priest.

The priest will say:
What will become of him
Who took life
Like a glass of champagne
And him with the broken tooth?

* Primo Carnera (1906–1967) – Italian boxer and 1933 world champion.

17

Autumn on parade

Autumn in nature and autumn in our faces.
The sultry breeze enfeebles, the glowering sun
Oppresses the ailing spirit in our breasts,
Shrivels the life trembling among the twigs of a poplar.

The yellow colours twirl in the final dance –
(a frantic desire of leaves dying one by one).
Our joys, passions, our last desires
Fall and are trampled one by one into the autumnal mud.

An oak-tree, reflected in a tear of heaven,
Tosses and bleeds in gigantic passion.
'To live! I want to live!' – it fights for breath,
Piercing the storm with cries of grief.

The horizon drowned in fog, joins in
The lamentation. In prayer dejected fruit trees
Fold imploring branches – but in vain, they know
Tomorrow they will die . . . Is there no hope anywhere?

The eye is saddened, saddened, too, the heart
At the hour of death, when silent fall the veins.
And from the grave to the highest heavens soar
Despairing cries of long-unheeded pain.

Autumn in nature and autumn in our faces.
Moan your desires, the off-spring of poverty,
Groan in mourning, weep over the corpses,
Which adorn the autumn among the withered branches.

Scandalous song

A pale nun who with the sins of this world
Bears my sins, too, on her weary shoulders,
Those shoulders, pale as wax, which the deity has kissed,
Roams the streets like a fleeting angel . . .

A pale nun, cold as a marble tomb,
With eyes the colour of ashes, the ashes of spent desires,
With thin red-ribbon lips, tight pressed to smother her
                                                            sighs,
A chilling image left me long after she passed.

From pious prayers she came and back to prayers she goes.
In down-cast eyes, in tight-pressed lips, in folded hands her
                                                            prayers repose.
Without her prayers what fate would be the world's?
But they cannot stop another day from dawning.

Oh, nun so pale, who makes love with the saints,
Who burns in ecstasy before them like an altar candle,
And reveals herself to them . . ., the saints I envy,
Pray not for me, for I am hell-bent by desire.

You and I, oh nun, are two ends of the one rope,
Of which two teams tug one against the other –
The struggle is stern and who knows how it will end,
So, tug the rope, let the teams contend.

Resignation

We have found consolation in tears . . .
Our heritage in life has been
Misery . . ., for this whole world
Amidst the universe is a grave,
Where the condemned being cowers,
His will crushed in the grip of a giant.
– An eye adorned with pure tears of deep pain
Shines from the far side of hell,
And sometimes the reflection of a fleeting thought
Flashes round the globe
To give vent to terrible wrath . . .
But the head hangs, the sad eye closed
And through the lashes wells a crystal tear,
Rolls down the cheek, splashes on the earth,
And from every droplet of the tear a man is born.
Each one on his own course sets out,
In the hope of the smallest victory; he roams from land
to land,
Over roads covered with brambles, along which he sees
Graves washed in tears and crazy folk who laugh.

Fragment

On the mercy of the merciless
The little beggar survived.
His life ran its course
In dirty streets,
In dark corners,
On cold doorsteps,
Among hypocritical faiths.
But one day, when the world's pity dried up
He felt in his breast the stab
Of a new pain – the hatred
Fired by want
In the hearts of the poor.
And – yesterday's little beggar,
Today became something else.
Like an avenger of old.
He conceived an imprecation
To pronounce on the world . . .
His throat strained
To bring out the word
Which his rage had stifled
And which died on his lips . . .

But speechless he sat there,
At the corner of the street,
The wheels of passing cars
Quickly ran over
And . . . silenced him.

New spirit

Eagle with a broken wing! Oh, wounded soul!
Groaning with the undiluted pain of your tormented breast!
Oh, suffering soul, sacrificed on a new altar,
Cry of the poor, of a brother in agony.

Eagle with a broken wing! Oh, soul in anguish!
Stand up! Stand proud like a noble lord,
The golden sun on your brow, the azure sky in your eye.
Resist! Cry out your misery – you still have the strength.

Oh, poor tender dove! Harbinger of the new ideal,
Pull the arrow from the wound and fly again
Above the storms of life, whispering kindly words of comfort,
Heal the wounds of those in want and give them hope in life.

But silence, the stricken soul is silent in affliction,
Grieving in self-pity . . ., oh, what bitterness!
It looks at a suffering world, looks at its wounds
And sheds a sparkling tear . . . alas, a star has died.

The themes

Is there the motif of a poem 'midst fading memories?
'Midst happy memories of childhood's innocence,
When untroubled by the world one romps
Heart filled with dreams, desires and hopes?

Amidst nearer memories of headstrong youth
Is there the motif of a poem of love
With resounding rhymes and ardent vows
Full of the lust for life and cries of joy?

On the pallid faces of fallen women
Who to sell themselves in doorways loiter,
On their faces a tragic poem is written
With tears and complaints that rise to heaven.

In dark corners where the instant laughter
Of a man crazy with desperation
Is echoed by his wife, son and daughter,
There in revolt great themes await creation.

From secret places in which dwells dread,
Whence life destroying passivity is spread,
There in betrayal a theme has its source
And with it the poet develops his verse.

Throughout a man's life themes of all kinds
Come and go endlessly. But the ultimate theme
To our minds brings terror – a paling of the face,
An ominous shadow – and the death knell tolls.

The weight of destiny

Fate oppresses us and turns us into worms,
We two-legged creatures who discovered the Divine
And then entangled matters even more . . .
Want to turn our falcon spirits into doves.

(But wait, oh, falcons? Why become doves?
In that life beyond the grave the gnats of paradise
Will pester you – and then in anger
You will roar . . . So, why become doves?)

Our cruel fate – the sword of Damocles.
How so? Are all our efforts doomed to fail?
Ah, life for us is gloomier than hell.
Neither truth nor falsehood ever helped the Earth.

Truth and falsehood? – precious jewels.
With them the world you buy and sell at will,
But think not you can alter its rotation . . .
No, it prefers to stagger blindly on.

Stagger to the right side, stagger to the left . . .
Like some poor clown who cannot keep his balance,
Since he broke his leg performing acrobatics –
His life is bitter without one drop of sweetness.

Song of the West

Song of the West, song of man drunk with self-confidence . . .
Song of another faith, with other temples and solemn rites,
In the apotheosis of iron, the souls pass through smoke-stacks,

Which whistle their derision at the old god and the sky,
And with dense clouds of filthy smoke blot out the sun.
Another faith, the mad faith of the marvellous West . . .
Man exalted staggers in senseless delirium.

He heeds the voice of his religion, wounds the sky,
                                            pierces the earth,
Rips the white horizons, strips nature, tears off her robe.
His creed, the creed of nakedness! Her mystery no longer
                                            troubles his brain.
He buries it and a sign of scorn or honour places on the grave.

Song of the West, song of man drunk with self-confidence . . .
His song is fine, winging on the hope of another life
In which the sun will change its course to rise in the West
– but oh! From happiness the world has lost its head.

With a tango of joy he already tangles the threads of the old guard,

And will scandalize the faithful on other planets.
Song of the West, song of man drunk with self-confidence . . .
Let us hear this song which is wrapped in clouds of steam
                                            and beads of sweat.

Esad Mekuli

(1916—)

Widely considered to be the father of modern Albanian poetry in what was once Yugoslavia, Mekuli was born not in Kosovo itself but in the legendary Montenegrin village of Plavë on the Albanian border where national traditions are still held high. He attended school in Pejë (Peć) on the Kosovo side of the wild Rugova canyon and studied veterinary medicine at the University of Belgrade. There he came into contact with Marxist teachings and subsequently took part in the partisan movement of World War II.

In 1949, he founded the literary periodical *Jeta e re* (New life) whose editor-in-chief he remained until 1971. Mekuli (pseudonym *Sat Nokshiqi*) is a committed poet of social awareness, whose outrage at social injustice, violence, genocide and suffering mirrors to a certain extent that of pre-revolutionary Migjeni of Shkodër. His first verse collection, *Për ty* (For you) (Prishtinë, 1955), was dedicated to the people of Kosovo. In addition to subsequent volumes of masterful verse, *Poetët e Bagdallës* (The poets of Bagdalla) (Prishtinë, 1966), *Avsha Ada, vjersha nga ishulli* (Avsha Ada, verse from an island) (Prishtinë, 1971), *Vjersha* (Verse) (Prishtinë, 1973), *Midis dashurisë dhe urrejtjes* (Between love and hatred) (Tiranë, 1981), *Brigjet* (The hills) (Prishtinë, 1981) and *Drita që nuk shuhet* (The light which does not go out) (Prishtinë, 1989), Mekuli has published translations of much Yugoslav literature, including the works of the Montenegrin poet-prince Petar Njegoš (1813–1851), as well as Serbian translations of many volumes of Albanian literature.

Longing for the unobtainable

Like lambs on the hillsides clouds frolic on high
As a longing for the unobtainable permeates my being:

How I long to join in the dance of the crimson clouds
And soar to the dazzling heights
In the rapture of a pastoral song . . .

And when the moonlight floods the valleys
Casting silvery rays upon ears of corn,
And the earth calls out in nocturnal desire,
Let me go
And visit
The extremities of my suffering and the haunts of my anguish.

Alas! My heart yearns
To join in the dance of the crimson clouds –
For my youth to exalt and rejoice
And for my aching heart to burst with longing.

But why does my heart beat with nostalgia,
                                        like a quivering voice,
And fear plunge into the depths of my heart and soul?

Whenever I contemplate the clouds over the city,
Whenever a longing for the unobtainable permeates my being.

Turk, elhamdulila*

The Turks took up the sword,
Europe trembled, shuddered.
And we too in Kosovo fought
For our beloved freedom.

They attacked with fire and sword,
For centuries our freedoms were lost,
The tyrant overran us:
'You are a Turk, elhamdulila!'*

Religion and nation were the same,
Moslem and Turk were one.
He wanted us to forget our very names:
'You are a Turk, elhamdulila!'

He forbade our language too,
To speak no Turkish was to be an infidel.
It is the word of God, they told us:
'You are a Turk, elhamdulila!'

'You are a Turk, you are a Turk,' they thundered
At the Albanians for centuries,
And one day one of us uttered:
'I am a Turk, elhamdulila!'

But no, Turks we are not!
Never! Let everyone know
We have always been Albanians;
Religion cannot wipe that away!

No, Turks we are not!
But their working people we love.
After times of blood and gloom
We shall go forth – hand in hand!

* 'Praise be to Allah'

Is it the Albanian's fault?

[1938. On hearing of the secret agreement to expel
four hundred thousand so-called 'Turks' from
'southern Serbia' to the wilds of Anatolia,
65 Kosovo students (56 Serbs and Montenegrins,
8 Albanians and 1 Turk) signed and published a
protest (in Serbo-Croatian and Albanian) against
the Yugoslav government for this crime against
the people. The protest was transmitted illegally
to foreign embassies in Belgrade and distributed
throughout Kosovo and Macedonia.]

Is it the Albanian's fault that he lives under this sky,
Under this sky, in the land of his ancestors?
Is it his fault that he exists and will not be uprooted,
The Albanian, slave or master, who wants to belong to himself?

Is it the Albanian's fault that his eyes flash fire
When he glares as others expel him from his home and his soil?
Is it his fault that he exists when others wish him dead,
Or that he will spill blood to defend his hearth
                                    and not give up alive?

Is it the Albanian's fault that he wishes to live as others do,
Like a human being, among his own people, now and forever?
Is it his fault that, despite force, he resists
Under the precious sky of Kosovo, the land of his ancestors?

Martin Camaj

(1925–1992)

Born in Temali in the Dukagjin region of the northern Albanian alps on 21 July 1925, Martin Camaj is an emigre writer of significance both for Albanian literature and for Albanian scholarship. He received a classical education at the Jesuit Saverian College in Shkodër and studied at the University of Belgrade. From there he went on to do postgraduate research in Italy, where he taught Albanian and finished his studies in linguistics at the University of Rome in 1960. From 1970 to 1990 he served as professor of Albanian studies at the University of Munich and lived in the mountain village of Lenggries in Upper Bavaria until his death on 12 March 1992.

Camaj's academic research has concentrated on the Albanian language and its dialects, in particular those of southern Italy. He began his writing career with poetry, later devoting himself increasingly to prose. His first volumes of classical verse *Nji fyell ndër male* (A flute in the mountains) (Prishtinë, 1953) and *Kânga e vërrinit* (Song of the lowland pastures) (Prishtinë, 1954), were inspired by his native northern Albanian mountains to which he never lost his attachment, despite long years of exile and the impossibility of return. These were followed by *Djella* (Djella) (Rome, 1958), a novel interspersed with verse about the love of a teacher for a young girl of the lowlands. His verse collections *Legjenda* (Legends) (Rome, 1964) and *Lirika mes dy moteve* (Lyrics between two ages) (Munich, 1967), which contained revised versions of a number of poems from *Kânga e vërrinit*, were reprinted in *Poezi 1953–1967* (Poetry 1953–1967) (Munich, 1981). A selection of his poetry has been translated into English by Leonard Fox in *Selected Poetry* (New York, 1990), as well as into Italian by Francesco Solano in *Martin Camaj – Poesie* (Palermo, 1985) and into German by Hans-Joachim Lanksch in *Gedichte* (Munich, 1991).

My land

When I die, may I turn into grass
On my mountains in spring,
In autumn I will turn to seed.

When I die, may I turn into water,
My misty breath
Will fall onto the meadows as rain.

When I die, may I turn into stone,
On the confines of my land
May I be a landmark.

To a modern poet

Your road is good:
The Parcae are the ugliest faces
Of classical myths. You did not write of them,
But of stone slabs and of human brows
Covered in wrinkles, and of love.

Your verses are to be read in silence
And not before the microphone
Like those of other poets,

The heart
Though under seven layers of skin
Is ice,

Ice
Though under seven layers of skin.

The old deer

The shepherds abandoned the alpine pastures
For the warmth of the lowland valleys,
Sauntering down the trails, talking loudly
About women and laughing
Beside the water of the stream bubbling forth
From well to well.

The old deer raised its head from the scorched earth
And observed the pale foliage. Then
It departed to join its sons,
They too with their minds on the does.

Broken, it too abandoned the alpine pastures and followed
The merry murmur of the stream below, a fiery arrow,
The wanderer in search of warmer pastures and winter grass
Which it will never touch!

When they slew it, the shepherds pried its eyes open
And saw in the pupils
The reflection of many deer drinking water from the stream.

Mountain feast

Blood was avenged today.
Two bullets felled a man.

Blood was avenged today.

Under the axe-head
The ox's skull bursts by the stream.
(Today there will be great feasting!)

Blood was avenged today.

The wailing of men gone wild
Mingles with the smell of meat on the fires.
And the autumn foliage falls
Scorched on the white caps
At the tables, outside.

Night. At the graves on the hill
Fresh earth, new moon.

The wolves have descended from the mountains
And drink blood at the stream.

First elegy

When I am snatched
From the tribulations of age, steep like a cliff,
Feel no pain for me, Taze.
Stretched out on the bier,
A lamb ready for sacrifice.
Let the old women mourn over me that day
For their own people long since dead.

And one more request, my wife:
When my father died, we slaughtered two oxen
To feed the starving – and the ants of the threshing-floor
With breadcrumbs.
But I shall die amidst people who are
Always full,
So at my wake serve
Only bitter coffee.

Fatos Arapi
(1930—)

Fatos Arapi was born in the port city of Vlorë. He studied economics in Sofia, Bulgaria, from 1949 to 1954 and worked in Tiranë as a journalist and as a lecturer in modern Albanian literature. Among his collections of verse are: *Shtigje poetike* (Poetic paths) (Tiranë, 1962); *Poema dhe vjersha* (Poems and verse) (Tiranë, 1966); *Ritme të hekurta* (Iron rhythms) (Tiranë, 1968); *Kaltërsira* (Blues) (Prishtinë, 1971); *Drejt qindra shekujsh shkojmë* (We're marching towards hundreds of centuries) (Tiranë, 1977); *Fatet* (The fates) (Prishtinë, 1979); *Poezi* (Poetry) (Tiranë, 1983); and *Duke dalë prej ëndrrës* (Leaving a dream) (Tiranë, 1989).
Child of the Ionian coast, Arapi has never lost his fascination with the sparkling waters of the sea, the tang of the salt air and the intensity of Mediterranean light, all of which permeate his verse. Indeed, beyond the echoing pathos of much of his revolutionary verse production on industrial and political themes, his true poetic vocation can be glimpsed in the creation of an equilibrium between the harmony of the waves and the rhythmic impulses of his being.

On the shoulders of my times

On the shoulders of my times
I rested my head.
I did not sleep. I did not doze.
On the shoulders of my times,
As on Her shoulder
                    I was lost in thought.

If I die young . . .

Like the linden tree, words spread their fragrance through
the twilight,
Deep in the words I have spoken,
As in the depths of the Ionian,
I see my face.

I feel no pity for myself,
I do not lament my fate.

And if I die young,
Do not close my eyes . . .
I wish no candles . . . just let me watch
The stars come out in the heavens above me.

If I die young.

Life

Life is a railway station of partings and meetings.
We are constant travellers,
Holding in our hands our inseparable baggage,
A little suitcase
Of struggles, onslaughts and memories.

I dived into the waters of the Ionian Sea

I dived into the waters of the Ionian Sea,
Into its hues and light.
I swim in a blaze of mirages,
Their sparkle captivates me,
Makes me quiver . . . And I feel:
Shooting through my soul,
Like azure currents of joy,
The very light and hues of the Ionian Sea.

Like azure currents of joy.

Do not hate me

Do not hate me.

The two of us were once
Like sky and sea:
If one clouded over, the other grew dark,
If one cleared, the other turned azure.
You and I were once
Like two logs on the fire:
Separated we died out,
United we raged.
But how soon love
Turned to hatred . . .

Do not hate me . . .

The workers

They are constantly entering poems,
                                    day and night.
They do not wait for the heavy gates to be opened
By intellectual love, by refined, delicate thinking.
They enter poems as they enter factories, plants,
Full of energy,
Noise and passion.
They ring the sirens, turn on the motors, begin work.
The façade of the poem resounds with drills, with lathes.
The grey, metallic air shudders with the vibrations.
They mount the scaffolding,
                                    the verses.
With the soldering-tool in hand they solder
                        iron and rhythms and tender rimes,
They test the calibres and the strength
Of our thoughts
                                    and of our loves.

Sultan Murat and the Albanian

Sultan Murat sat astride his stead
And observed the prisoner bound hand and foot:
His advanced age, his wounds, his chains . . .
'Albanian,' he inquired, 'Why do you fight
When you could live differently?'
'Because, Padishah,' replied the prisoner,
'Every man has a piece of the sky in his breast,
And in it flies a swallow.'

Dritëro Agolli

(1931—)

Dritëro Agolli is a writer who has had a far from negligible influence on the course of contemporary literature. He was born of a peasant family in Menkulas in the Devoll region near Korçë and finished secondary school in Gjirokastër in 1952. He later continued his studies at the Faculty of Arts of the University of Leningrad and took up journalism upon his return to Albania, working for the daily newspaper *Zëri i Popullit* (The People's Voice) for fifteen years. From 1973 to his retirement on 31 January 1992, he was president of the Albanian Union of Writers and Artists.

Agolli made his name originally as a poet before turning to short-story writing and is widely admired in both genres. His first verse collections, *Në udhë dola* (I went out on the street) (Tiranë, 1958), *Hapat e mija në asfalt* (My steps on the pavement) (Tiranë, 1961) and *Shtigje malesh dhe trotuare* (Mountain paths and sidewalks) (Tiranë, 1965), introduced him to the reading public as a gifted lyric poet of the soil and evinced masterful verse technique. One senses the influence of his training in the Soviet Union in this early verse, the spirit of Eduard Bagritsky (1895–1934) and Dmitri Kedrin (1907–1945) in particular. An attachment to his roots came to form the basis of his poetic credo, in particular in the volume *Devoll, Devoll* (Devoll, Devoll) (Tiranë, 1964). Despite his political career and his representative functions as head of the Union of Writers and Artists, Agolli, who delights in rhyme and unusual figures of speech, has managed to remain true to his rural roots. His fresh, clear and direct verse, coloured with the warm foaming milk of brown cows in the agricultural co-ops, with ears of ripening grain in the Devoll valley and with the dark furrows of tilled soil has lost none of the bucolic focus which remains the poet's strength, and one which he cultivates consciously.

The cynic's monologue

I loved you,
  I love you no longer!
    Worse can happen in life.
There are those who remain lovers
    until they grow old,
There are those who are lovers
    for but a month.
I loved you,
  I love you no longer!
    You were born to suffer,
      so suffer!
I am an honest man,
    I respect the truth.
There are those
   who do not love
    but lie
      all their life.
I am straight to the point
    and blunt in tone,
I tell you
  'I don't love you'
    on the telephone!

The petty bourgeoisie

What's all the uproar?
                  we can sit in the kitchen;
The food smells good, we won't go hungry;
If we are thirsty,
          we can drink;
If our nails are getting long,
               we can cut them!

The heart

Mountains, mountains, mountains,
Full of iron, heroism and grain!
No measure can contain you,
Only my heart, that has room for everything!

The cow

The cow chews her cud in the hay-filled barn,
I lean my face against her great flank
Feeling from her inner depths the warmth,
The warmth of hay gathered in the meadows.
Over her black horns hangs an electric light
Shining down into the pail of milk.
I cannot leave the cow.
With my face against her flank, I smell the foaming milk.
The milkmaid gently removes the pail
And waits a moment, her hands dripping.
She says:
    'Are you a vet?'
I lift my face from the cow:
      'No, a poet.'
She smiles and studies me with her blue eyes,
Lovely, wise and peaceful.
She reflects for a while and realises
I cannot write a line without a cow . . .

The vineyard

The rows of crates are lined up in the vineyard,
Crates where raki and exquisite wines lie sleeping,
Rows like lines of verse,
Sometimes scanned, sometimes free.

No one asks the grape-pickers
Why the lines are long or short.
It's enough if they produce
A heavy wine or a twenty-percent raki.

The foundations

Here are the foundations of my old house,
The house I left once upon a time,
And here too is the old doorstep,
More than a doorstep – a stone.
Tender grass has covered both the doorstep and the
                                                    foundations
And above the grass, apple trees wave their branches,
Trees unknown to me when I was a child,
Apple trees that friends planted the day of my departure.
Under the grass together with the chiselled doorstep
Sleep old verses from school notebooks.
They sleep and the dense grass grows over them,
The apple blossoms cast their petals.
Visions of these one-time verses come alive
Whenever the road brings me back here,
And they rustle with the grass and apple leaves
And flutter past . . .
Then I sit down under a tree and talk to myself,
A blade of grass between my lips:
It is true that I have written poems in the city,
But deep down inside I am a farmer . . .
And I need not blush at having hung onto this lifeblood,
Lifeblood of good dreams,
Upon which I have built other dreams,
Beautiful, delirious dreams . . .

First nostalgia

'You who leave your first hearth,
Do you know that it burns with fiery nostalgia?'

On the boulevard I stop for a moment in silence
In front of my old apartment building.
There is light in the windows
Where someone else now lives happily.

Greetings, brother, I say to myself,
Looking in the windows from afar,
From the trees along the pavement a leaf
Falls onto the collar of my jacket.

So many years I lived there in peace and in excitement,
Where the lights are shining in the windows tonight.
I wrote many poems and articles,
Got married and raised children.

How many sleepless nights I spent
Pondering over my notes and books,
And entertaining friends who arrived at the door,
Entertaining them leisurely and hospitably.

And my friends – wise, noisy, audacious,
Read whatever I had written
With pleasure or turning up their noses,
Saying, 'We expect real verse!'

And who knows how often with them
I took to the roads of Albania!
To hell with the kitchen, cups and saucers and spoons,
Let us look for verse together on our way!

And again with books and notes
I returned to that small apartment,
With my trousers full of burrs,
And juniper needles in my hair . . .

On the boulevard I stop and light a cigarette
In front of my old apartment building.
The glow in the windows burns with a first nostalgia
That can never be moved elsewhere.

In the ancient city

The two of us stroll through the ancient city,
With its many windows and orchards,
From every window we hear a ballad,
From every portal we hear a poem.
Can you feel the sound of a verse?
It comes with a warm breeze from the city's ancient past,
It comes from the mouths of statues sleeping under the
                                                    doorsteps,
And under the roots of vines hanging from the trellises.
Had you come two thousand years ago,
The ancient sculptors
Would have fashioned you in Alpine marble
And you would have slept under the foundations of a
                                                    doorway,
Undiscovered for a long time,
And I would have arrived two thousand years later
To discover you and carry you off in marble
                                    to the Art Gallery . . .
Don't laugh!
That is certainly the way it would have happened.
How fortunate it is that you were not born two thousand
                                                    years ago
And that we could now meet.
In my arms you will be warmer
Than as a statue in the gallery.

A couple of words to poets to come

We had no time to write of love
Though we were impetuous lovers,
The country needed songs of freedom,
The country needed songs of grain ripening in the fields.
The country demanded of us poor poets,
That we teach courses to fight illiteracy,
That we build dams on the rivers,
That we light the flame of socialism in the mountains.
Do not wonder, oh poets yet to be born,
And do not judge us for what we have not accomplished.
Compared to you, we will look like simple monks
Laden with grain and heavy iron chains.
We, who spent many a sleepless night,
We, who accomplished many a great deed,
Could we not at least have written a couple of love poems,
Could we not have stammered, 'Oh, my beloved?'
Do not believe we were heartless! If only you could have seen
The passions we felt for the girls we loved and heard
What sweet nothings we whispered in their ears on those
                                              radiant
Evenings! But we lacked the time to publish those sweet
                                              nothings.
Our printers were busy with more important things.

Work

Under his nails the dirt was dark blue,
Dirt from the fields and meadows,
Blue like the lines on the globe,
Like the strings of a violin.
Nor can it be washed out
With soap and water in the bath.
Dirt entered the furrows of those hands silently
Like a plough breaking through the soil.
I know those warm fingers,
Those good fingers.
My father's nails were blue with dirt
Even as he lay in his coffin.
He looked as if he were not dead at all,
But simply dozing before setting out for the fields
And he would do at dawn,
Lying back with his head in the palms of his hands.

Vorea Ujko

(1931–1989)

Vorea Ujko, pseudonym of Domenico Bellizzi, is among the most popular and respected of the Arbëresh (Italo-Albanian) poets. Ujko was a modest priest from Frascineto (Alb. *Frasnitë*) in Calabria who taught modern literature in Firmo (Alb. *Firma*) where his memory has been cherished since his death in a car accident in January 1989. Ujko's verse, a refined lyric expression of Arbëresh being, has appeared in many periodicals and anthologies as well as in seven collections, four of which were published in Italy, two in Albania and one in Kosovo. Vorea Ujko is a poet of rich tradition. He is the worthy heir of the great nineteenth-century Arbëresh poets Girolamo De Rada (1814–1903) and Giuseppe Serembe (1844–1901), both of whom he admired very much. His verse is intimately linked with the Arbëresh experience, imbued with the *gjaku i shprishur* (the scattered blood). Though devoid of the lingering sentiments of romantic nationalism so common in Albanian verse and the standard motifs of exile lyrics, Ujko's poetry does not fail to evince the strength of his attachment to the culture of his Balkan ancestors despite five hundred years in the *dheu i huaj* 'foreign land'. His verse collections include: *Zgjimet e gjakut* (The awakening of the blood) (Castrovillari, s.a.); *Kosovë* (Kosovo) (Cosenza, 1973); *Mote moderne* (Modern times) (Schiavonea, 1976); *Ankth* (Anguish) (Prishtinë, 1979); *Stinët e mia* (My seasons) (Corigliano Calabro Stazione, 1980); *Këngë arbëreshe* (Arbëresh songs) (Tiranë, 1982); *Burimi* (The source) (Tiranë, 1985); and *Hapma derën, zonja mëmë* (Open the door, mother) (Tiranë, 1990).

Arbëresh moment

I love the Byzantine bell-tower,
Against the azure sky
That pierces straight into our souls
As evening turns to violet
And the girl of my dreams
Chats on the doorstep,
With lowered head.
In my solitary reverie
There appear before me
Scenes of my childhood
And the tragic face of Garantine.
From the distant shades
Comes Constantine's steed galloping*
On its funereal course.
And an Arbëresh echo
Pierces the air and transfixes my heart,
Rising aloft like a mystery
On its weightless wings,
Seizing the ivy on the wall,
Seizing the silence,
Seizing my blood.

* Constantine and Garantine are figures of Albanian and Arbëresh folklore.

Arbëresh song – X

A great dawn awaits you
And you will find the words
That you do not use now.
It will be a bright dawn
And everything will sing out in the sunshine –
The vineyards, the river, the house,
Your swelling heart
Will sing out in the sunshine.
You are a strong root
And your army has no foot soldiers
For they are all captains.
Greetings, my brother.

You are beautiful

You are beautiful, girl,
But love between us
Is impossible
Because, just between the two of us,
I once loved your mother
Who was beautiful, like you.

Three maidens

Three fair maidens,
Three maidens, three sisters,
Three embroidered wedding-dresses.
The youngest said
Love will come,
It will come with the dawn.
Suddenly death came
And took her away.
Two fair maidens,
Two maidens, two sisters,
Two embroidered wedding-dresses.
The second said
Perhaps death will come
And only you will remain.
Soon love came
And took her away.
And now I wait alone.

Music

I listen to the music of the night
When waves fall,
All colours faded
And the moon descends
Behind the trees.
I am not at home here
Yet neither do I feel foreign.
I will kiss the brow
Of the girl who knocks at the door
And asks in my language
If I'd like some coffee.
Perhaps she thinks
I have learnt the language
To use it on my travels,
And does not know the secret
Of our blood ties.

Din Mehmeti

(1932—)

Din Mehmeti is among the best-known classical representatives of contemporary verse in Kosovo. He was born in 1932 in the village of Gjocaj i Junikut near Gjakovë (Djakovica) and studied Albanian language and literature at the University of Belgrade. He now lectures at the teacher-training college in Gjakovë. Although he has published some prose, literary criticism and a play, he is known primarily for his figurative poetry which has appeared since 1961 in twelve volumes. Among his most recent collections are: *Ikje nga vdekja* (Flight from death) (Prishtinë, 1978); *Zogu i diellit* (The sun-bird) (Prishtinë, 1982); *Fatin tim nuk e nënshkruaj* (I shall not seal my fate) (Prishtinë, 1984); and *As në tokë as në qiell* (Neither on earth nor in heaven) (Prishtinë, 1988).

Mehmeti's verse is one of indigenous sensitivity. He relies on many of the figures, metaphors and symbols of northern Albanian popular verse to imbue and stabilize his restless lyrics with the stoic vision of the mountain tribes. Despite the light breeze of romanticism which transfuses his verse, as critic Rexhep Qosja once put it, this creative assimilation of folklore remains strongly fused with a realist current, at times ironic, which takes its roots in part from the ethics of revolt in the tradition of Migjeni (1911–1938); and Esad Mekuli (1916—). Mehmeti's poetic restlessness is, nonetheless, not focused on messianic protest or social criticism but on artistic creativity and individual perfection.

Din Mehmeti

The light still blazes

You are stronger than the five centuries
That have besieged your fortress

You are the crux uniting all resistance –
A place where the bells of war resound

A fire that melts fraternal hatred,
A sun offering its rays to our blood vessels

A cradle from which arise
The lullabies of love and adjuration
Scanderbeg

With you we have penetrated even into the heart of the atom
With your sword – flashing across the heavens

With its fiery pronouncement – root of our mother tongue,
On the long road behind the light that still blazes
Over the fortress
Scanderbeg . . .

Olympus

The streets of Athens did a brisk business
With the visitors

Homer where is Penelope?

Brothels enticed travellers
Into the folds of the underworld

The tainted beauties
Played with instincts
And with the shadow of misfortune

Homer where is Penelope?

And letters torn up at the door,
A mournful cry –
Lament of a life sold out . . .

Homer where is Penelope?

(Athens 1976)

Dialogue with the lake

The lake has grown dark
The lake has gone mad

May my bark hold

On this side are your cliffs
Of bones
On the other side immortal dreams

May my bark hold

You once searched for a way out
In your heart

The cape of hope is far

The blood-red flowers
Will arrive

May my barracks hold.

Dhori Qiriazi

(1933—)

Born in Kolonjë in southern Albania, Dhori Qiriazi studied at the Faculty of History and Philology of the University of Tiranë and then turned to teaching.  His early poetry appeared in the Albanian literary journal *Nëntori* (November), and he has subsequently published several verse collections: *Kur zemra rreh së pari* (When the heart first beats) (Tiranë, 1958); *Ballada intime* (Intimate ballad) (Tiranë, 1963); *Poema e ushtarit* (A soldier's poem) (Tiranë, 1968); *Pisha me kristale* (The crystal torch) (Tiranë, 1971); and *Vitet* (The years) (Tiranë, 1982).

Oh, first love

Oh, first love, oh spent youth,
If only your sweet breeze would come back to us once more . . .
Why did you come when we knew nothing of love,
Why were you gone when we burned with the flames of passion?

The leafy acacias are disrobing

The leafy acacias are disrobing
And hoar-frost has covered the fields,
The road is now deserted
Where we first met one another,
The withered leaves linger in sorrow
Blown by the wind.

No more will we meet on that road,
The sad acacias will fall silent,
Will tremble in the north wind
And whiten under the flakes of snow,
And yet it will remain alive
To await us evermore!

The wind blows, the acacias are disrobing!
And rain beats against the window-panes,
The wind blows and the body shudders,
The road is now deserted . . .
But feelings do not fall like the leaves.
No, feelings will not wither like leaves.

Dhoria Qiriazi

I have noticed . . .

I have noticed: whenever a storm rages,
The poor little birds cower and tremble,
Only the eagles spread their wings to the wind . . .

Fahredin Gunga

(1936—)

The enthusiasm characteristic of Kosovo poetry of the sixties can be seen in the early works of Fahredin Gunga (1936—) born in Mitrovicë. Gunga studied in Belgrade and now works for Rilindja Publishing Company in Prishtinë. His first volume of verse with its perfected, harmonious rhythms, *Pëshpëritjet e mëngjezit* (Morning whispers) (Prishtinë, 1961), which appeared the same year as the first poetic collections of Din Mehmeti, Adem Gajtani and Ali Podrimja, was elegaic in tone, not without a certain obsession with deception and death. Subsequent volumes have shown him to be a poet of searching, though at times with nebulous ideas, whose abstract symbolism and abstruse metaphors often take an unexpected surrealist turn.

They include: *Mallkimet e fjetuna* (Dormant curses) (Prishtinë, 1970); *Kepi i Shpresës së Mirë* (Cape of Good Hope) (Prishtinë, 1973); *Psalmet e gurta* (Stone palms) (Prishtinë, 1977); *Nokturno për Orkidenë* (Nocturne for the orchid) (Prishtinë, 1981); and *Mallkimet e zgjuara* (Awakened curses) (Prishtinë, 1985).

The wave

Burning with desire for the rocks
She breaks like a woman in orgiastic frenzy
And carries in her arms the joy of remoteness,
The mock tale of beauty, and

Born of the womb of the sea
Like the bastard child of unnamed sin
Pregnant with the weight to deceive life, and

Like a thief she snuggles onto the breast of the rocks
Into the rugged embrace of the old warrior, and
She lies and lies, and

Lying is the game of the waves,
– the game of falling and rising,
Of death and of birth, and

She startles at the frigidity of the rocks,
What deception as she makes love with the centuries! . . .

The porter

Oh, how hard this land is,
How often my heart has been crushed under the saddle!
Oh, how hard this land is! . . .

Night is fairer than day,
It rocks you to sleep, brings memories.

Sir,
Grant me but one smile,
Like those of my childhood,
And for once don't just look at my back.

Ismail Kadare
(1936—)

Ismail Kadare is at present the only Albanian writer to enjoy a broad international reputation. His talents both as a poet and as a prose writer have lost none of their innovative force over the last three decades.

Born and raised in the museum-city of Gjirokastër, Kadare studied at the Faculty of History and Philology of the University of Tiranë and subsequently at the Gorky Institute of World Literature in Moscow until 1960 when relations between Albania and the Soviet Union soured. He had begun his literary career in the 1950s as a poet with verse collections such as the modest *Frymëzimet djaloshare* (Youthful inspiration) (Tiranë, 1954) and *Ëndërrimet* (Dreams) (Tiranë, 1957), which gave proof not only of his 'youthful inspiration' but also of talent and poetic originality. His influential *Shekulli im* (My century) (Tiranë, 1961), helped set the pace for renewal in Albanian verse. *Përse mendohen këto male* (What are these mountains thinking about) (Tiranë, 1964), is one of the clearest expressions of Albanian self-image under the gruesome years of the Hoxha dictatorship. Kadare's poetry was less bombastic in form than earlier verse and it thus gained direct access to the hearts of the readers who saw in him the spirit of the times and who appreciated the diversity of his themes. In the sixties, Kadare turned his creative energies increasingly to prose, though he never abandoned poetry completely, as evinced by his subsequent verse collections *Motive me diell* (Themes with sun) (Tiranë, 1968), *Koha* (Time) (Tiranë, 1976) and *Buzëqeshje mbi botë* (Smiles on the world) (Prishtinë, 1980). He has indeed helped to bridge the gulf between poetry and prose.

Poetry

Poetry,
How did you find your way to me?
My mother does not know Albanian well,
She writes letters like Aragon, without commas and periods,
My father roamed the seas in his youth,
But you have come,
Walking down the pavement of my quiet city of stone,
And knocked timidly at the door of my three-storey house,
At Number 16.

There are many things I have loved and hated in life,
For many a problem I have been an 'open city',
But anyway . . .
Like a young man returning home late at night,
Exhausted and broken by his nocturnal wanderings,
Here too am I, returning to you,
Worn out after another escapade.

And you,
Not holding my infidelity against me
Stroke my hair tenderly,
My last stop,
Poetry.

(Yalta, 1959)

Childhood

My childhood – ink-stained fingers,
Bells in the morning,
The muezzin at dusk,
Collections of cigar-boxes and old stamps,
Trading one Ceylon
For two Luxembourg.

Thus they passed,
Childhood days,
Chasing after a rag-ball, raising dust and cries,
A rag-ball,
Made of grey Albanian rags.

(1958)

And when my memory

And when my fading memory,
Like the after-midnight trams,
Stops only at the main stations,
I will not forget you.

I will remember
That quiet evening, endless in your eyes,
The stifled sob upon my shoulder,
Like snow that cannot be brushed off.

The separation came
And I departed, far from you.
Nothing unusual,
But some night
Someone's fingers will weave themselves into your hair,
My distant fingers, stretching across the miles.

Longing for Albania

I was filled with longing for Albania
Tonight as I returned home on the trolley,
The smoke of a Partizani cigarette in the hand of a Russian
Curled bluish, twirled upwards
As if whispering to me, its compatriot,
In the language of the Albanians.

I long to stroll through the streets of Tiranë in the evening,
Where I used to get into mischief,
And through the streets where I never got into mischief.
Those old wooden doorways know me,
They will still hold a grudge against me
And will snub their noses at me,
But I won't mind
Because I am filled with longing.
I long to stroll through the lanes full of dry leaves,
Dry leaves, autumn leaves,
For which comparisons can so easily be found.

I was filled with longing for Albania,
For that great, wide and deep sky,
For the azure course of the Adriatic waves,
For clouds at sunset ablaze like castles,
For the Albanian Alps with their white hair and green beards,
For the nylon nights fluttering in the breeze,
For the mists, like red Indians, on the prowl at dawn,
For the locomotives and the horses
That huff and puff, dripping in sweat,
For the cypresses, the herds and graves
I was filled with longing.
I was filled with longing
For the Albanians.

I was filled with longing and swiftly journey there,
Flying over the mists, as over desires.

79

How far and how beloved you are, my country.
The airport will tremble with the droning,
The mists will hang in suspense over the chasms.
Surely those who invented the jet engine
Must have been far from their country once.

(Moscow 1960)

The cataracts

The cataracts cascade downwards
Like spirited white horses,
Their manes full of foam and a rainbow of hues.

But suddenly, at the edge of the gorge,
They fall on their forelegs,
They break, oh, their white legs,

And die at the foot of the rocks.
Now in their lifeless eyes
The frozen sky reflects.

The old cinema

Old cinema,
Abandoned cinema
Where no films, not even reruns, have been shown for a
                                        long time,
Where the audience no longer makes a clatter with
                                        their seats,
Where peanuts are no longer sold
At intermission.

The stained screen,
The broken speakers,
The empty seats like lines unwritten.
Pensive and full of nostalgia
I stare from the doorway
At this poem of seats, long and abandoned.

Childhood cinema,
Tumbledown cinema,
I've seen so many countries,
I've seen so many auditoriums,
But none of them have I entered with such joy
As you,
Shabby old cinema,
Wonderful and precious to me!

Nowhere have I felt better,
Not in luxurious halls of shining velvet,
With a couple of blondes at my side.
To you I come
In the company of a gypsy or two.

Coins, coins,
Money collected with difficulty,
Jingling merrily at the ticket-booth,
The posters by the mosque
And by the Bazaar Cafe
Drawn by Qani the doorman himself.

One poster said:
'Soviet film',
Another for the same film said:
'Czech film',
But no one really cared,
We forgave you everything,
Dear old
Cinema.

On that bit of screen
We saw a bit of the whole world,
For the first time.
On six square metres
The world had no limits,
The world was splendid
Even though the screen was patched up.

We too were patched up,
Patched up was the Republic,
Time, elbows, states were patched up,
But the glossiest of screens
Had never seen
A sparkle like the one
In our eyes.

Old cinema,
Abandoned cinema,
Seats where childhood days
Sat in rows.
Childhood days,
Always chattering,
Like a row of birds
On a telephone wire.

Old cinema,
Abandoned cinema,
Heavy, long and sunken seats.
As old as I get,
Wherever I go,
Like a porter I'll carry them
With me, those seats.

Train timetables

I love those train timetables at little railway stations,
Standing on the wet platform and contemplating the infinity
of the tracks.
The distant howl of a locomotive. What, what?
(No one understands the nebulous language of steam engines)

Passenger trains. Tank cars. Freight cars full of ore
Endlessly pass by.
Thus pass the days of your life through the station of your
being,
Filled with voices, noise, signals
And the heavy ore of memory.

Requiem for Mayakovsky

I ate at the same table with his assassins
At the writers' vacation house
in Dubulti, in Yalta.

They smiled and talked of socialist realism,
While his blood
spattered their car windows,
Their jackets, armchairs, salaries
And the ruddy face of the critic Yermilov.

They thumped their chests and talked of socialist realism
In the presidial chamber of red velvet
under the emblem with a star,
While the Russian winter
froze him,
Stretched out upon the black earth,
only to be thawed out in April.

Obscure forces dressed in socialist garb,
A pack of lousy critics, speculators, careerists,
Took up the attack with the age-old refrain of the mediocre:
'You were great, but we got you.'

There stands his bronze statue in Mayakovsky Square,
It rose and glumly observed the years to come.
Behind the crowd of his assassins, whom he knew,
He saw the first clouds of the counter-revolution darken
the sky.

What are these mountains thinking about

1

What are these lofty mountains thinking about
As the sun sets in the distance beyond the highway?
A mountaineer sets out at the fall of night,
His long rifle
Casting a hundred-mile-long shadow on the ground.

The shadow of the rifle hurries
Over mountains, plains, villages;
The shadow of its barrels hastens through the dusk.
I too set forth along the hillside
With a thought in my mind
Somewhere.

The shadow of the thought and the shadow of the rifle
Cross and collide in the twilight.

2

This is how you have always set out, Albania,
On your long legs
And with a long rifle.
You wandered without knowing where to go,
Onwards toward the morning full of clouds and mist,
Grey and ponderous, as though born of night.

3

Cloudbursts ate away at the land
And bared the bases of the cliffs.
Thus, the centuries have gnawed away at your body
Until your very sinew and ribs were exposed.

Sinew, sinew and ribs,
Only boulders, rocks and mountains,
Little flatland,
Oh, how very little flatland
The centuries left you!
The centuries gnawed at you like hounds
Wherever they could get at you.

When you met them
They attacked you,
The teeth of time
Dug into your thighs,
But you did not turn back,
You did not yield.

4

You never removed the long rifle
From your shoulders,
From shoulders covered in wounds,
From shoulders of skin and bone.

You ate bread in brine,
Brine and maize every night,
And you saved a little fat,
Oh, that little bit of fat
For friends and for the long rifle,
To grease the long rifle.

Women give birth to children,
But a rifle gives birth to shots,
And the two have been equally sacred
To the Albanian:
The shots and the children.

The child will tomorrow take to the plough
And the rifle will protect him at night.
Time fired shots over the shoulders of Albania
Like rice thrown over the shoulders of a bride.

5

The pealing of bells
Rung by night
Resounded over the mountain slopes.
What were the bells saying,
What were the priests murmuring
To their high churches
In their foreign tongues?
Latin logic, in long sentences,
Strove to bend the long rifle.

6

And there were poets
Poised on handcarved furniture
From your forests
Who, inspired by you,
Wrote of varnished furniture
And of nightingales
In the trees, ancestors of furniture,
Who had once sung.

They forgot
That in your forests,
From whence the furniture came,
There were many wolves
And few nightingales.

7

Storms, fever, malaria ravaged your body,
The priests and the mullahs
Deafened you.
Like Saturn,
You devoured your children in blood feuds,
And on these feuds the minarets and belltowers
Bestowed their blessings.

8

And fierce enemies nipped at the borders,
Nipped at the pale, bare shoulders of our native land.
The land arose, tottering,
Its eyes glowing with hunger and fever
And, forgetting its hunger,
Set forth in the night to measure the borders,
With a foot-rule?
With a yard stick?
No,
With the long rifle.

9

Your first contact with inventions,
With the new technology of civilization
Was with types and calibres of new weapons,
Which were tested against your withered, bullet-riddled
breast.

After the fighting
There remained but the solitary graves of mountaineers,
Mounds of melancholy,
Monosyllabic names,
For a long time
Nothing but a heap of stone
And, instead of flowers at the head,
A monotonous song
Chanted by the tribe,
A monotonous song.

And beside the long limbs
The rifle fell away, the long rifle.
And after the long limbs
The short name fell away,
The letters dropping off
Like pine-cones in the rain,
And after everything else
At last the song ceased,
The montonous song of the tribe.

10

And once again Albania cowered in a hut
In her dark mythological nights
And on the strings of a lute strove to express something
Of her incomprehensible soul,
Of the inner voices
That echoed mutely from the depths of the epic earth.

She strove to express something
But what could three strings
Beneath five fingers trembling with hunger express?

It would have taken hundreds of miles of strings
And millions of fingers
To express the soul of Albania!

11

If one was slain on a hillside,
Another would arise elsewhere,
As if out of the earth –
The gaunt Albanian,
And above his body,
Like an iron limb,
The long rifle
Rose black.

With the rifle in his hand,
He wandered through these regions,
Over mountains and plains.
The rifle made him taller,
Though it often made his life shorter.

12

Chewing on legends in the freezing night,
Famished, you ate your own songs,
Albania.

You were overcome by sleep,
Bent over the plough at twilight
Under the dark heavens
And you dreamt of so little joy
As no one had ever dreamt of before.

You dreamt
Of one more slice of bread,
Of one more spoonful of brine.
You dreamt of brine and bread
And of a little, so very little fat
To share with the rifle.

Your wedding was
Lightning in the midst of your misery,
Full of nerves, drums, quarrelling
And a little joy,
The little joy you dreamt of behind the plough.

13

The nights gave birth to mornings,
Ponderous and grey;
The days cursed the nights,
The nights cursed the days.
Albania in her ruggedness
Gave birth to beautiful children,
Implanting in each child
A dream, a hope.
Tending her withered breasts,
Albania gave life,
She gave birth to soldiers,
Who later died in the sands of the Sahara,
Singing of the Bridge to the Kaaba.

14

The sons you sent to the cities of Europe,
Who knew foreign pleasures,
Returned

One by one,
To find a sorrowful land,
Clouds laden with yellow rain.
The monarchy, like a quarryman, smashed their dreams.
They arrived
With suitcases full of illusions
Under the shadow of minarets, of monasteries,
And rambled in autumnal delusions
Until the earth returned them to her bosom
And they rotted under the monotonous song of the rain.

15

Early fruits are expensive in price,
But early fruits are often destroyed by frost.
Albania placed them back into her bosom
'It is still too early,' she said,
Observing the gloomy light of dawn.

16

And once again she bent over the plough
And sowed her bitter tears in long furrows.
Under a sombre sky of endless ignorance
She sowed her tears
For rainstorms and tempests to come.

17

Amen!
The priests and a few drowsy poets came forth
To declaim abstract genealogical glories,
But you trampled on traditional laws
With your bare feet and scratched their poetic figures.

As if you were some insane beauty,
The traitors spun you around to take advantage of you,
Shouting,
'No worry,
No matter if you have no food.

We are God's chosen people,'
While you scratched out an embossment under the stars,
Your embossment of scabby, filthy sores.

18

The poets wrote hymns to the fairies and nymphs,
Who were delousing themselves by the streams.
You could count the very ribs of the fairies, the nymphs,
Who, for a few coins, would proffer themselves in the bushes.

On occasion, the fairies and the nymphs managed
To abandon their epic alpine meadows
And descend one by one
Into the villages.
And, one by one, they ended up
In the bawdy-houses,
In the bawdy-houses that dotted
The weary mountain ridges,
Like wounds,
Like derision.

19

The nymphs departed,
Abandoning the myths,
And the myths began to empty.
The myths,
The last granary of the nation,
Returned to the abandoned churches.

For the myths, like people, were hungry,
And lived in great poverty,
Greater than any other,
In an age when the winds of boredom whistled
Over deserted mythical plains.

20

In the palace, King Zog gave nightly balls,
The princesses smiled,
The dancers waltzed.
In the quiet cells of frigid monasteries
The priests studied suffixes.

The orchestra played on
In Café Kursaal,
The elderly matrons powdered their noses,
While pregnant Albania
Miscarried the days
On bloodstained diapers of clouds.

21

And the mountain ranges were silent like horse caravans,
Oh, what caravans they were,
These mountain ranges!
They waited for hours,
For days,
For months,

For someone to lead them into the great battle,
For someone to lead them to a new world,
The mountain ranges waited with their heads in the clouds.

22

There were those who tried to tug at the mountains,
Like at the halters of horses
And led them a little way down the road,
But in the dark, they lost their way.

The formidable mountain ranges wandered in circles
Through the night and the fog,
Blind,
Terrified.

94

As if frightened by a tragic shrieking of old,
The heroic mountains neighed in their dreams.

23

And thus they turned in circles like a caravan in the desert,
Until they settled down, calm once again,
Until twilight, the fortresses, hunger, the epic legends
Jumped on their backs again,
And with them
The bawdy-houses too.

But the calm was deceptive,
The long mountain caravans were waiting,
Waiting for a leader,
Albania was waiting
For the Communist Party.

24

What are these lofty mountains thinking about,
These enigmas of ridges stretching north and south?
I continue on my way
In the shadow of the long rifle,
That long rifle:
Your Archimedes' lever, Albania.

Through the sight of his rifle
The Albanian observed the horizons and the times,
The solitary whistling of his musket
Forced the centuries to duck.

This rifle barrel
On the Albanian's back
Has grown there like a long sharp bone
Transplanted into his spine by a difficult destiny,
An extension of his backbone,
This awesome iron limb,
A proud atavism of ancient times.

Ismail Kadare

The fearless Albanian has crossed the centuries,
With destiny on his back,
Trudging in his ancient sandals
Across the ageless land holding the graves of our forefathers.

This land which has brought forth
More heroism than grain through the ages,
This land . . .
That is what these lofty mountains are thinking about,
As evening falls in the distance beyond the highway.

(1962–1964)

Azem Shkreli

(1938—)

Azem Shkreli is an admired Kosovo Albanian poet and writer of short stories and novels who was born in the Rugova mountains near Pejë (Peć) in 1938. Now head of 'Kosovo Film Studios' in Prishtinë, Shkreli is an intellectual poet who, though highly expressive, is by no means verbose. His experience among the rugged hill tribes of the Rugova district at the foot of the 'Mountains of the Damned', and his observations of their traditional wisdom and way of life, are given new significance by his urban perceptions. Critic Agim Vinca has described him as a poet of ideas and profound judgments. Azem Shkreli (not to be confused with writers Adem Shkreli and Ymer Shkreli) is the author of  seven volumes of verse, one novel, a volume of short stories and drama. His verse collection *Kënga e hutinit* (The call of the owl) (Prishtinë, 1986) has been translated into English by John Hodgson (Prishtinë, 1989).

At Saint Naum's

I have come here
To be baptized without a name.

I have come here
To be blessed without a crown.

I have come here
To be sanctified without incense.

I have come here
So that two roads may cross.

I have come here
To pray to mankind on behalf of God.

Mass

Let my grass grow above my head
Above my head let my grass grow
My grass above my head let it grow

Let it grow
Let my grass grow above my head

Over Europe

Evening. We are in flight, plucking at the wool
Of the clouds. Beneath us a white kingdom
Azure triumph. We speed on and pay no heed
Borders armies herds

As if on the century's crest we push aside
The mildew of history the wars as if they had not been
A lady shakes the sighs from her handkerchief
Somewhere over Mauthausen

I look out the window. I do not know why I laugh
While slowly emptying the bottle with my friend
Who will be born there below us tonight
Merchants? Sartre? Generals?

Evening. We are in flight. Beneath us pensive
Europe drowses over serious matters
Sleep on wise lady I never bothered
About your whims which were not mine.

Tale about us

The prime of life
We ate unripe fruit

In the branches remained only
The bird's voice and feathers

Summer passed and all drank
Its red wine

One got drunk, one
Fell on the horn of a goat

One clambered onto its strong-willed
Head to see what time it was

The wisest one prayed to God
And the devil not to pray for us

Portrait

He placed
His thoughts on the table and
Pondered

A man of the world

He extracted the seeds
From his own watermelon head
One by one

A man of the world

Rugovë

I am returning
To your harsh beneficence
I am returning

I am returning
To your savage beauty
I am returning

Once again
I am to meet you
Like a mother

Rrahman Dedaj

(1939—)

Rrahman Dedaj is a poet in constant evolution and one who has contributed substantially to the modernization of Albanian verse in Kosovo. Dedaj was born in 1939 near Podujevë before becoming executive editor of Rilindja Publishing Company. His poetic works are characterized by rich, emotive expression, by an almost mathematical precision in structure and semantics and by a search for a balance between tradition and modernity.

Dedaj's first collection *Me sy kange* (With eyes of song) (Prishtinë, 1962) evinced both personal and social motifs. In *Simfonia e fjalës* (Word symphony) (Prishtinë, 1968), his sensitive lyrics took on more neoromantic tones, not unlike those of his fellow Podujevan poet Adem Gajtani (1935–1982) in many ways, with an Orphean world of blossoms and butterflies. Later volumes, in particular *Baladë e fshehur* (Hidden ballad) (Prishtinë, 1970), *Etje* (Thirst) (Prishtinë, 1973) and *Gjërat që s'preken* (Things intangible) (Prishtinë, 1980), inaugurated a new stage in Kosovo verse, more atune to contextual symbols and myths. This neosymbolist verse often runs rampant with animal and plant metaphors. caught up and preserved in disciplined, elliptical structures. His recent collections, *Jeta gabon* (Life makes mistakes) (Prishtinë, 1983) and *Fatkeqësia e urtisë* (The misfortune of wisdom) (Prishtinë, 1987), have been devoted more to historical and literary themes.

Our word

You slept in our pierced bone
You wove legends and temples you toppled

Bloodstained bridge between ashes and light
Rebel child of the heart, bread and salt

Adorned bride with girlish dreams
Veil never torn in white 'kullas'*

You have threaded your name through yellow rings
Your love has been hunted with bow and arrow

Like the full moon you are born in every love
And build your home in every heart

Crimson butterfly in our bone
We have immured you as a song extracted from our flesh.

* Kulla: fortified stone mansion of the northern Albanian Alps.

When . . .

When we dream of the dead
They say it will rain,
When we dream of heroes
Our bones begin to grow.

Obstinate verse

It strives to be born
It has no head.

If it came out of another head
It would forget
The pain which nourishes it.

If it came out without a head
They would give it a number
Instead of a name.

A number which people
Would add and subtract
Multiply and divide
Always mistakenly.

Between

Between stone and stone
Bread.
Between bread and bread
Word.
Between word and word
Thirst.
Between thirst and thirst
Flower.
Between flower and flower
Name.
Between name and name
Bridge.
Who stole the hills?

Rrahman Dedaj

The dog

He chases after lightning
The rain cannot drench him

He will find his friend

He circles the black tree
Stone-still in his own shadow

He will find his friend

A bat swoops
To touch his head

He will find his friend

A^{li}
Podrimja

(1942—)

Ali Podrimja was born and raised in Gjakovë, a beautiful Kosovo town known for its artisans and the purity of its Albanian. Like many other Kosovo Albanian literati of his age group, Podrimja studied Albanian language and literature in Prishtinë. He is considered by some to be the most typical representative of modern Albanian verse in Kosovo and is certainly the Kosovo poet with the widest international reputation.

Podrimja's first collection of elegaic verse, *Thirrje* (The calls) (Prishtinë, 1961), was published while he was still in secondary school in Gjakovë. His second volume, *Shamija e përshëndetjeve* (The handkerchiefs of greeting) (Prishtinë, 1963), followed in more or less the same vein. *Dhimbë e bukur* (Sweet pain) (Prishtinë, 1967), a title reminiscent of Migjeni's 'proud pain', introduced new elements of the poet's repertoire, a proclivity for symbols and allegory. Subsequent volumes up to the mid-seventies, *Sampo* (Sampo) (Prishtinë, 1969), *Torzo* (Torso) (Prishtinë, 1971), *Folja* (The verb) (Prishtinë, 1973) and *Credo* (Credo) (Prishtinë, 1976), proved him to be a mature symbolist at ease in the wide range of rhymes and metres. After *Sampo 2* (Sampo 2) (Skopje, 1980) and *Drejtpeshimi* (Balance) (Prishtinë, 1981), his collection *Lum Lumi* (Lum Lumi) (Prishtinë, 1982) in particular marked a turning point in contemporary Kosovo verse. Dedicated to the author's deceased son Lumi, this collection introduced an existentialist preoccupation with the dilemma of being, with elements of solitude, fear, death and fate. Podrimja' volume *Fund i gëzuar* (Happy ending) (Prishtinë, 1988) is yet another outburst of his Sisyphean obsession with the destiny of mankind, his unceasing and ironic attempt to grasp the needle of existence in a haystack of allegorical dichotomies – the past versus the present, the peripheral versus the nuclear, myth versus reality, the specific versus the general.

Ghazal

My salvation
Your body, oh woman,
A green meadow.

My health
Your body, oh woman,
Scorching noon on a branch.

My hatred
Your body, oh woman,
Evening fallen on its knees.

Oh woman, oh woman, deep sea.

The unknown

What a beautiful bird
But the hunter

    blind
and mute

Go back to Homer's verse

Go back to Homer's verse
Go back to where you came from
This is not your age go back
Free men from themselves
And shadows free them from masks
And flights free them from insomnia
And silence free them from fever
And rain this is not your age
Go back to Homer's verse
Troy has fallen and long has it been
Since men have sung the Marseillaise

Rain in a legend

If I throw a stone into the river
Silence runs a fever

If I sing an ancient song
Silence is overcome by insomnia

If I look for myself in a game
Silence has a headache

It rains and rains
In a legend now and forever

The black cat

On my journey
A black cat follows me

And my soul says to me
You'll get stuck half way

And the song says to me
You'll never sing me aloud

And the light says to me
Look for me awake

So come and say the word
When you don't know whom you love or hate

Come and believe the face in the mirror

A black cat follows me
On my journey

It will dictate the final hour

The illness of my family

for my father, Hamzë Podrimja

My father God bless him died of a stomach ulcer
Before having his say about Love and Mankind
My mother God bless her thrice was operated in the Hospital
Thrice the Wolf howled around our house
A tumour in my brother burst into madness
He gave up the ghost beside a fountain when no one was
                                                                    watching
My sister we buried three metres deep
In the shade of a poplar we buried her one summer's evening
With all the pus of a filthy world
I, I shall wander a planet drowned in dreams
Farther and farther I shall flee from the blood and the self
If my nerves are altered in the tambourine of time
Oh illness of my family
Confounded game
Of fate.

Requiem

Night burnt out in my eye
Gives up the ghost
In alleyways

Somewhere in a forest somewhere in a poem
Howls the wolf
Wants to devour the sky, the earth

Over the crooked roof
Burns the moon
Radiant

And the song of confused birds
Ends deep
In the world of dreams

Mother
Oh mother interminable pain

The day of the butterflies

Under the lids of your eyes
Somewhere perished
The day of the butterflies

My cry
Has slain
The drousing distances

The day of the butterflies
Perished somewhere
Under the heavy lids
            of your eyes

Mother
Oh mother
interminable pain

Between two ages

Between two loves
You live

Between two fires
Burns the memory of you

Between two words
Rises your monument

Between two ages
I search for you

Mother
Oh mother interminable pain

Ballad of man

I know a Man
He wanders naked through the world

Instead of a tie
He binds a serpent around his neck

Instead of a shirt
He puts on a wolf's skin

All the time
He is undressing, undressing

In a public place

No one sees him
And he wanders naked through the world

A Man who has lost everything

Feelings
Eyes

The stolen flame

How did the serpent bite him?

He said to the Lion: quiet!
The Lion knelt before his sword.

The people said: it's been a long time
Since we've seen such a spectacle in our circus.

But how did the serpent manage to bite him?

In our town the children now report
That he went to get the flame
And that one rainy day the people stole it from him.

And how did the serpent bite him?

He said to the Lion: quiet!
And the Lion knelt before his tenebrous eyes.

And you dead

It was summer
Overhead the sun
Shadows, you around Europe

From that horrible journey
You returned one day with eyes wide open
You entered your father's poem without knocking

There you are in safety Lumi
I swear no harm
Will come to you

It was summer
The sun in the west
And you dead and

It is the Albanian's fault

It is the Albanian's fault
Who breathes
And walks on two legs.

I who take tranquillizers
And swat flies all the time
In the toilet.

It is the Albanian's fault
Who besmirches his own wife
And frightens my family.

The apple my hand cannot reach
On the highest branch,
With dead words he filled
The well.

It is the Albanian's fault
That not more of Turkey exists,
More of America or Norway.

      The Gulag which is so far off.

That they chose me and sent me
To sniff him out.
Does death smell?

It is the Albanian's fault
All the more that he does not eat
Or fall asleep.

That our sewers are broken
And the catacombs of the Balkans
Have fallen into ruins.

It is the Albanian's fault
Who sketches his own face under the moon
And breaks windows and stirs up muddy water,

Who speaks Albanian, who eats Albanian,
who shits Albanian

It is the Albanian's fault
The Albanian is the one at fault
For all my undoings

And for my broken tooth
And for my frozen laugh
So therefore: BULLET

Ha ha ha
Ha ha
Ha

May God have mercy!

Xhevahir Spahiu

(1945—)

One of the most talented of the new generation of Albanian poets is Xhevahir Spahiu from Skrapar in southern central Albania. Spahiu's verse is energetic, uncompromising and intense. At the same time, he is a poet of precise nuances, hues and shades of meaning. He is the author of five collections of verse: *Mëngjes sirenash* (Siren morning) (Tiranë, 1970); *Vdekje perëndive* (Death to the gods) (Tiranë, 1977); *Agime shqiptare* (Albanian dawns) (Tiranë, 1981); *Nesër jam aty* (I'll be there tomorrow) (Tiranë, 1986); *Tek rrënja e fjalëve* (To the roots of words) (Prishtinë, 1988), and *Kohë e krisur* (Mad age) (Tiranë, 1991), and much more is certain to follow in the years to come.

History

The blood dripped and grew roots in the stone,
We wiped the blood off the swords with our thick
                                        white flanel,
When we had no weapons
We would pluck out one of our ribs
And make a sword of it.

For you

Love is present in full.

In these eyes
In these words
In the brief silence between them is love.
And even before the two of us were born,
I was waiting for you! Waiting for you!
                          Waiting for you!

The eagle

Out of the azure heavens
      the eagle swooped down one day
Onto the flag.

The heart
      said to the hand: carve!
And the hand carved it in stone.

The eagle
      from its refuge in the cliffs
Penetrated the expanses of song.

Penetrated
      the hero's breast
And replaced the heart.

To be with you

To touch your silence as one touches an object,
To stare deep into those eyes,
Where love drifts like a boat
And not to want to be with you forever?

To walk with my arm around your shoulders
And not to feel the roar of the blue waves,
Lemon-trees over my head?
The boats like fires in the night?

To be with you,
To laugh with you,
And not to understand that the sea
Is trying to escape its own conch?

To be with you?
To be with you!

Sunday taxis

At the station under the pines twenty-seven taxis
Are waiting in silence this rainy night.

Tomorrow they will cross the city again
Like the raindrops on my brown coat.

What journeys await them? And what do they dream of,
These taxis sleeping in the neon light?

In their metallic dreams mingle the reflections
Of lives which tomorrow will cross one another's paths.

Some will be ridden by real loves,
In others the victims of matchmakers will weep.

If I knew which taxi the tears would ride,
I would throw my body under the wheels to stop it.

The foxes

One evening I was studying the cypresses:
Fair,
Elegant.

Suddenly I seemed to see
Foxes hiding underground
The wind was bending their protruding tails . . .

Why did I think of you foxes?

Maybe because cypresses are always planted
Near idols,
Near temples!

Our history

The blade of the sword we came down in a dash.
The sword then came down upon us in a flash.

Agim Vinca
(1947—)

Agim Vinca is a leading poetry critic and poet from Veleshtë near Struga in Macedonia whose popular lyrical verse is firmly anchored in the soil of his place of birth and of his childhood. He finished school in Struga on Lake Ohrid and studied Albanian language and literature at the University of Prishtinë where he taught contemporary literature until expelled in September 1991 by the Serbian military. Vinca is the author of the verse collections *Feniksi* (The phoenix) (Skopje, 1972); *Shtegu i mallit* (The path of nostalgia) (Prishtinë, 1975); *Në vend të biografisë* (In lieu of a biography) (Tiranë, 1977); *Buzëdrinas* (Inhabitant of the lower Drin) (Prishtinë, 1981); and *Arna dhe ëndrra* (Patches and dreams) (Prishtinë, 1987). He has also published noted works of criticism, in particular *Struktura e zhvillimit të poezisë së sotme shqipe (1945–1980)* (The structure of the development of contemporary Albanian poetry 1945–1980) (Prishtinë, 1985) and *Orët e poezisë* (The poetry hours) (Prishtinë, 1990).

Becoming a poet

To be an oasis in the wilderness,
Not to forget there are many who thirst in this world.

To be a lantern in the darkness,
Not to forget there are many blind in this world.

To be a ship in the waves,
Not to forget that forgotten masses are waiting on the banks.

To say pig to the pig and Socrates to Socrates
And drink your part of the poison.

To write an open letter to the Lord
And list all your sins.

To dig your own grave on the highest mountain peak
And turn into a rod of lightning.

Biography of the root

Who knows when you were born,
In what age, in what place?

Who knows when you sprouted,
On what hill, in what dale?

No one can measure your age,
In years, in seasons.

The teams,
The experts
Search in vain.

You are like life itself.

Your branches,
Twigs,
Buds grow.

Your trunk thickens like a sauce,
You refine the flavour
Without worrying about theories, origins,
Expertise, diagnoses . . .

A strong root. Stubborn.
Ancient. Young.
Homeland.

Albanian rhapsody

Have you been to the source of the Black Drin,
To Saint Naum, in the south?
Have you seen how its waters flow
Like a gentle lyric poem.

Have you been to the source of the White Drin,
To the North Albanian Alps, among the mountain cliffs?
Have you seen how its waters roar
Like epic verse.

Have you been to the source of the Black Drin
To Ohrid, to Struga?
Have you seen how its waters weep
Like a clarinet at twilight.

Have you been to the source of the White Drin
To Radavc near Pejë?
Have you seen how its waters quiver
Like the strings of a lute.

Have you seen how our rivers flow
Through the gorges and mountains,
Have you heard their melodies:
Albanian rhapsody

Psalm for Saint Naum

You are too beautiful
To be true

You are too sinful
To be holy

An azure curse
Slumbers in your eyes

How I pity you!

Ballad of the Dry Mountain

There is a mountain in the south
Between two lakes
They call the Dry Mountain

And no one can tell you
How this mountain
Stays dry surrounded by water

Nearby is a meadow
With the startling name
The Meadow of Tears

And no one can tell you
How this mountain
Stays dry near the tears either

There is a mountain in the south
Between two lakes
They call the Dry Mountain

And no one can tell you
Why this mountain
Always thirsts near the water

Dry Mountain
No grass, no trees, no birds
Dead for the living.

Like a human being
Withered from desire.

The names

For a friend

For our children
We have chosen beautiful names,
Good names:
Drilon,
      Shkumbin,
Gramoz,
      Korab,
Vjosa,
      Valbona . . .
May they flow after us
Like our rivers,
May they rise above us
Like our mountains.

My dead

First of all my mother died,
Then my sister,
Now recently my father.
I was left motherless,
I was left sisterless,
I was left fatherless.
But we have been reunited
Because I –
Cannot live without them.
I cannot live
Without my dead,
I don't want to
       I don't know how.

The hounds of Sodom

First they bite,
Then they bark.
The hounds of Sodom!
A bizarre race.

Who can tell
When they wag their tails
As a sign of friendship;
When they gnash their teeth
As a sign of menace.

First they bite,
Then they bark
(They bite by night,
They bark by day) –
An ancient habit
Of their pedigree.

They treat the living
And the dead the same:
They dig up their bones,
They lick clean their guts.

It's always the same.

The hounds of Sodom,
A noble race!

Eqrem Basha

(1948—)

Kosovo poet Eqrem Basha was born in Dibër in western Macedonia and studied Albanian language and literature at the University of Prishtinë. He was editor of the drama section of Prishtinë television until expulsion, and is author of ten volumes of verse, including most recently: *Atleti i ëndrrave të bardha* (The athlete of white dreams) (Prishtinë, 1982); *Udha qumështore* (The Milky Way) (Prishtinë, 1986) and *Brymë në zemër* (Frost in the heart) (Prishtinë, 1989). Basha has also translated the works of Sartre, Ionesco, Camus and Malraux into Albanian.

Introduction to the meaning of solitude

There is somewhere an abandoned house
With cracked walls and sagging roof
In its yard the grass unmown
Unswept dust the door unmoved

Guarded by a dog

A small forgotten man
With unshaven beard and unkempt hair
Paces back and forth like a madman
Lost face hope abandoned

Looking for his dog

Silence

A living landscape
Then
A glass
A photograph

In this landscape
I am the only moving
Object

As quiet as a mouse

I listen to my own silence

Perpetuum mobile

A wave of anger seized me
And caused me to foam

I later regretted it

But the next day
I wanted

To foam again

Road with an end

The world does not know its limits
But I know
Mine

The world has no limits
It starts here
And stops here
But I have them
I who play
With its greatness

Woe

Surrogate

We suffer from the same disease
We strive for salvation in the same manner

We love and are loved the same way
We love and burn the same way
We count our wounds

You suffered from the same disease
Now I burn
You are dead
And have left me
A piece of your suffering

Natasha Lako
(1948—)

Natasha Lako, poet and novelist from Korçë, is one of the more prominent representatives of the first generation of women writers in Albania. She has published the following volumes of poetry: *Marsi brënda nesh* (March within us) (Tiranë, 1971); *E para fjalë e botës* (The world's first word) (Tiranë, 1979); *Këmisha e pranverës* (The spring shirt) (Prishtinë, 1982); *Yllësia e fjalëve* (Constellation of words) (Tiranë, 1986); *Natyrë e qetë* (Quiet nature) (Tiranë, 1990); and the novel *Stinët e jetës* (The seasons of life) (Tiranë, 1976). She has worked for 'New Albania' Film Studios in Tiranë and is active in politics.

Natasha Lako

A woman's monologue

Which eyes am I to use to see you, love,
Which eyes?

They were difficult years,
The veil extended right to our feet
And hindered our every movement.

We had much to throw off,
We had much to pick up.
Suddenly out of the darkness
A new day dawned.

It was the dawn we chose therefore,
The time of day which disperses all things.
With its light
We created new eyes.

The leaves fall every autumn

The leaves fall every autumn,
In autumn every day, every hour . . .
And with the fall of leaves in the courtyard
The wind begins to count the minutes of the year.

Grandmother sweeps the leaves,
She sweeps and sweeps . . .
She senses every year that grandfather is back
To shake the trees
And sit out in the wind.

The leaves begin to lose their colour,
The leaves grow mute,
As grandmother sweeps and sweeps . . .

Insomnia

A clear night has fallen with its soft, supple body
Upon the great city.
The lofty trees converse with the moon
And flowers bend and doze.

The streets descend into an asphalt slumber
And dream of tomorrow's footsteps,
From the lamp-posts incandescent light shines down
Upon the fallen leaves and steps of passers-by.

But the calm is not real,
I know people are not asleep –
Young mothers are raising children in their wombs,
Even in their deepest sleep.

At night, after threshing

Somewhere,
The rolled copper wire
(inside it is the colour of roasted grain)
Is carrying the signals of your voice.

The light of day descends behind the horizon
(it is the hour when children curl up and go to sleep).

Your call from the forests
Came down to me on the plains like a rustling . . .

(Somewhere,
A receiver suddenly looks
Like a bird pecking at clear signals of joy,
Like grains of wheat.)

This evening, great expanses reunite us
Much better than any means of communication . . .

Albania

Albania, red flower –
Half budding, half open.

Albania, storm bird –
With a nightingale's voice and an eagle's wings.

Albania, song for a hero –
Both a war cry and a lullaby.

Natasha Lako

I shall write a poem about the doorstep

I shall write a poem about the doorstep –
Smooth, simple,
Exposed to the winds and the rain
And still untouched.

Nothing can cover up the doorstep,
Everything remains light,
And when an Albanian places his foot on it
It is like a dance.

Legends and weddings have crossed it,
Poems and festive songs,
But never has an enemy
Poised his foot on these two handbreadths of life . . .

The grave of Paul Eluard

In the sky an endless swarm of birds
in flight.
Down below,
Like a bird made of earth
his grave.

All around are imposing monuments
to politicians,
to statesmen.

Flowers
Are the only monument
to the poet.

Oh, what new verdure

Oh, what new verdure,
Perhaps a day old, perhaps an hour,
                    perhaps a minute.
If it were a baby, it might cry
When exposed to the wind.

But it rustles, it murmurs
                    unassumingly
Breast-fed
From the depths of the earth.

Oh, what new verdure,
Perhaps a day old, perhaps an hour,
                    perhaps a minute.
Billions of years, billions of centuries
                    have penetratèd this foliage . . .

Bardhyl Londo

(1948—)

Bardhyl Londo from Lipë near Përmet has built up a reputation as a leading Albanian poet of the eighties. He studied language and literature at the University of Tiranë, taught for some years in his native district of Përmet and now works for the literary journal 'Drita'. Londo's lyrics depart from the concrete: details and moments of existence he has experienced, lived through intensely and transformed into verse in a controlled, erudite manner. His poetry, which is written in standard metres and mostly rhymed, melodiously echoes the rich traditions of Tosk verse to the extent that Tiranë critic Razi Brahimi has placed him at the crux between the classical Rilindja poet and thinker Naim Frashëri (1846–1900) and the  influential poet of the soil Dritëro Agolli (1931—). His work has appeared in five collections: *Krisma dhe trëndafila* (Shots and roses) (Tiranë, 1975); *Hapa në rrugë* (Steps in the street) (Tiranë, 1981); *Emrin e ka dashuri* (They call it love) (Tiranë, 1984); *Vetëm Itaka* (Only Ithaca) (Prishtinë, 1989); and *Si ta qetësoj detin* (How can I calm the sea) (Tiranë, 1988), which was awarded the 1989 Migjeni prize.

The monuments

Along the streets,
               in schoolyards, city squares
They stand
          silent,
               pensive.
I call out to the passers-by
         like Leonidas to the Spartans:
Oh people,
       do not see but majesty
            in the monuments!

Here is a man transformed into bronze
He was once a warrior
         with quill and sword.
If you but touch him
His wounds
Will drip once again
With blood.

Here is a poet transformed into marble
He was once a simple man,
         he laughed and cried like a child.
Put your ear to his chest
His heart was broken
Out of anguish for you,
Oh people!

Blood-paved road
       life of a phoenix . . .
Do not see but majesty
        in the monuments!
Since they had a life
       full of tribulation
Let us make eternity easier
For them.

And let your heart beat a little faster, oh passer-by.
Do the best you can

When you look them in the eye,
And if you cannot
              become a monument
                  yourself,
Be worthy
Of your fellow citizens!

Çajupi*

Send me a stone, a stone, he said
  as he died in distant Heliopolis.
There were others, others there were
  who demanded feather pillows.
With chapped and parched thirsting lips
  he dreamt of a drop of water from a fountain.
There were others, others there were
  who sipped their whiskies in a bar.
Vito quivered. Mara's tears dried:
  the eyes of the poet of grief had closed.
There were others, others there were
  who twirled like tops at a ball.
A sorrowful death, worthy of a great existence,
  eternity has now begun its journey.
There were others, others there were
  of whom we know neither when they lived nor died.
Nonetheless, may it distress us, brother,
  that we could send him no stone while he lived.

While he lived, while he lived, that we sent him not even a
             stone . . .

---

* Andon Zako Çajupi (1866–1930): poet and playwright of the Albanian community in Egypt.

Who are you?

Who are you? Challenge of the centuries,
Spectre of tyrants, terror of kings.
You demand freedom. Your rifle has no cock.
You long to fly and you spread no wings.
Dressed like a priest, you make fun of God.
Who are you? God or the devil?

At times Beethoven, at times Khayyam.
You know neither when you laugh nor when you cry.
Sweet Ophelia, raven that startles you.
That grieves you so and you know not why,
Sombre Hamlet, Sancho the joker,
Half ascetic, half sinner.

At times hatred, at times love.
Who are you? Fire or ash?
You love noise, you speak of silence,
Half jester, half king
Your feet in Boston, your heart in the Balkans.
One eye laughs, the other weeps.

Your hands are freezing, you are not on fire.
You drink of the rivers and die of thirst.
Deafening silence, thunder and calamity.
Who are you, who are you?
Oh, genius is indeed veiled in a dilemma,
Within a tear the man shines through!

Thus you scale the centuries:
Challenge of oblivion, terror of kings,
Singing fire, biting frost.
Who are you? Noli the Albanian!*

---

* Fan Stylian Noli (1882–1965): Albanian statesman, churchman, writer and translator.

Migjeni

Give me a wave –
                and I'll give you a river,
Give me a word –
                and I'll give you a song,
Give me a bird –
                and I'll give you a sky,
Give me a love –
                and I'll give you pain,
Give me a hope –
                and I'll give you a life,
Give me a fist –
                and I'll give you freedom,
Give me a dream –
                and I'll give you a future,
Give me a god –
                and I'll give you blasphemy.
Mi   (you
        gje   find
                ni   me)
                all this,
Mi
        gje
                ni
                and I'll give you a name:
                                        MIGJENI

Lasgush Poradeci

Death had forgotten him. Startled,
It lost its way in his fragrant verse.
The day he closed his eyes
The lake at Pogradec in disbelief froze over
Like one huge tear . . .

The poet's last request

If your eyes rest upon this verse and ponder,
I shall see
A fair vision.

If your eyes quiver, even for a moment, on reading this verse,
I shall resound like a guitar
All through the night.

If your eyes pass over this verse with indifference
I shall have found my death.

Do not forget to come to my funeral.

Chronicle of a love affair

On Monday we met. We said each other's names.
On Tuesday we became friends. We smiled.
On Wednesday we made love. We lost our way.
On Thursday we had an argument. We were saddened.
On Friday we reviewed the past few days like a film.
On Saturday we sought ways to find one another.
On Sunday we rediscovered our love, like Columbus.

And then it was Monday again.

Whenever

Whenever I walk past the drugstore
I shake like the leaf of a poplar in the autumn.
May you never enter it, my love,
May your hands never hold a prescription.

Whenever I walk past the hospital
I quiver like the broken string of a harp.
May you never take this road, my love,
May you never cross that threshold, my dear one.

Whenever I walk past the ambulances
I shudder at the thought that you might be in one.
May you never hear their sirens,
May you never know how swiftly they move.

Whenever I walk past cemeteries
. . . .
I never walk past cemeteries.

Ithaca

Ithaca slumbers under the September sky.
The olive trees are like women awaiting their tardy husbands.
I am filled with a longing for my home far away
For my wife in Tiranë who will not sleep tonight.

Help me, Ulysses! Cast off your legendary cloak!
Tell me something wise, something fervent.
Roads begin, get lost, run forth, disappear
More intricate than the stitching on Penelope's woven gown.

Roads, roads, roads . . .
To the east, to the west,
To the Ionian, to the Aegean.

The times are indeed modern,
But you can lose the thread again
As in the age of Ulysses.

Which one will take me to my Ithaca?
Which word will calm my waiting wife?
Far from the sirens of the sea screaming hysterically once
                                                              again,
Far from the Circes of the twentieth century!

I will not lose this road!
I will find it even blind!

We are all a little like Ulysses,
Even if we do not have a Penelope
We do have an Ithaca!

Morning on the Acropolis

The statues wipe their sleepy eyes.
(Can a statue actually sleep?)

Under the tunics,
Under the wreathes of laurel
The hearts of the thousand-year-old statues await a new day.

And look: over Lykabettos and over the chariot of Achilles
The sun-face of Glezos appears.

The thousand-year-old statues set off on their way.

Farewell, Manolis!

Feelings in search of Homer in Athens at midnight

Midnight loiters in the old quarters of Athens
Like a blind old woman not knowing her way.
Blind are the crossroads,
Blind
The monuments.

Lifeless are the eyes of the Acropolis statues,
Lifeless
The many-hued eyes of the traffic lights.

I am looking for you, oh great blindman.

And if I find you,
I will go blind myself!

Bardhyl Londo

Meeting with Leonidas

The freeway is silent,
The Aegean is silent
Like a body, paralysed and lifeless,

The trees,
The birds,
The clouds are silent.

There are only the two of us, oh great leader,
The two of us and this fair silence,
With no strikebreakers.

How will we understand one another then?

. . . Those of us who know the language of freedom
Have no need of an interpreter.

Thermopylae, September 1983

Only Ithaca remains

The ships have changed. They are no longer like those of
Ulysses.
The love affairs have changed. They are no longer like those
of Menelaus.
The women are different. They are no longer like Helen.

And again the successors will change over the centuries.

Only Ithaca remains.
Ithaca for the child, Ithaca for genius,
It, the eternal,
Dreams,
love,
life,
death:
Ithaca – man himself.

Moikom Zeqo

(1949—)

Archeologist Moikom Zeqo was born in the ancient port city of Durrës (formerly *Durazzo*, Lat. *Dyrrachium*) and studied at the Faculty of History and Philology of the University of Tiranë. He has worked for the Museum of Archeology in Durrës as well as for the Classical and Mediaeval Art Division of the Academy of Sciences and has recently taken up a political career. His highly intellectual verse has been inspired in good part by the lost grandeur of his ancient 'Dyrrachium'. Among his verse collections are: *Brenda vetes* (Inside oneself) (Tiranë, 1974); *Libër i hapur* (Open book) (Tiranë, 1986); and *Njëqind zemra* (One hundred hearts) (Tiranë, 1989). Zeqo has also published verse for children.

For Gabriel García Márquez

Even after a thousand years of solitude
The tree of the heart does not wither.

One day even flowers
Will grow on the moon.

We therefore believe
That the mythical autumns of the patriarchs
With their value-added nuclear sceptres
Are fossilized images.

You longed for pure air
Over the continents!

Your identity deriving from the titles of your books,
How many people your name contains!

The double

When the Roman consul Lucus Anitius gave orders
For the legions to march into the heartland of Illyria
He had not only a chronicler on his war council
But also a double of King Gentius,
Dressed just like him, with painted eyebrow
Most certainly with a false sceptre,
And with a sentence learnt by heart:
'I am Gentius, King of the Illyrians!'

The consul said to the chronicler that day,
'What happens to the real Gentius is of no consequence to the
Battle. We are the truth and shall spread it as we wish,
The tools of writing are the arms of victory too,
Words which the most distant of our descendants will read.
The shackles of Roman victories must not fall
Even though they are made of paper!'

When Lucus Anitius celebrated his 'Illyrian triumph' in Rome,
Riding his martial chariot and crowned with golden laurels
The double walked in front of him,
Moaning loudly, so as to be heard by all:
'I am Gentius, King of the Illyrians!'
The masses roared and made fun of the captive.

The official chronicle attributed to the ancient spectacle
'Universal' significance!

Anna Comnena

When the Emperor Alexius uncovered the plot
Of his ambitious daughter, Anna Comnena,*
Princess of Byzantium,
He cut her hair and made her a nun.
She thereafter took to writing on parchment
And chronicled the startling history of the century,
Of the city of Durrës, the Norman sieges,
Of Komiskortes, hero of the Arberians.
Anna Comnena, princess of Byzantium,
Her hair shorn, grown old over her writings,
Wrote of the beard of Bohemund Guiscard
Which the people of Durrës had once insulted in public!
And this was all of greater value
Than her dreams of power.
Condemned to live the life of a nun,
She wrote and devoted herself to her times.

* Anna Comnena (1083–ca.1153): Byzantine historian.

Antigonia

Pyrrhus the Great razed many a city,
Destroyed temples, toppled statues of kings,
He rivalled death itself,
And surpassed destruction by fire.

But for his wife, Antigonia the fair,
For whom his love was indestructible,
Pyrrhus the Great ordered that a whole city be built,
High up on a mountain, as close as possible to the sun,
In expanses reserved for the gods alone,
Such was his desire to immortalize in the light
The so mortal face of his spouse.

He gave a whole city
The name of his wife who had passed away
In the unrelenting progress of time.
For the first time
He laid foundations,
Built squares where children would frolic,
Dug wells that would never dry up.

So much the old warrior achieved,
So much death's rival accomplished.

Only this time,
In the name of life!

Antigonia, 10 June 1985

Moikom Zeqo

On my elderly aunt

She is elderly, wears thick eyeglasses
Knows nothing of telescopes,
Sees clearly into hearts, memories, beyond time.
She is elderly, terse in her speech,
With old sayings,
Laconic gestures.
She is elderly and finds in her grandchildren
That which old age has deprived her of.

She is elderly, her hair has gone grey,
She does not like us mentioning her hair,
Like a poet editing out the clichés.
She is elderly and certainly knows nothing
About Archimedes' principle, about short circuits,
About the number π from elementary school,
About multiplication tables and DNA,
But she does know about bread, growing up and about
                                        children.
She is not the least interested in the secret of the metaphor
But does understand the chirping of the wagtails perfectly.
She is elderly, chats quietly
With her brother (my father) who has been dead for thirty years
Asks him questions, listens to him and replies.
This is more important than Homer's imagination
Which sent Ulysses on his voyage to the other world
And brought him back to life.
My aunt tells her secrets to the dead
Who visit her, drink coffee with her,
Tell her things.
It does not worry her at all
That they are preparing for her return visit.

My aunt is elderly, she very rarely says anything,
But knows the names of all her newly born grandchildren,
Dreams of them getting married,
In a quarter, a half or three centuries time.
She still keeps her wedding veil
With which to cover her face
The day we pay homage
To her absence so packed with life.

Sabri
Hamiti

(1950—)

Born in Dumnicë near Podujevë in
Kosovo, poet and critic Sabri Hamiti
studied comparative literature both
in Zagreb and at the Ecole Pratique
des Hautes Etudes in Paris, where
the demigods of French structural-
ism brought their influence to bear
on him. He finished his doctorate at
the University of Prishtinë. Hamiti is
the author of numerous volumes of
prose, poetry and drama, as well as
innovative criticism. Among his
most recent verse collections are:
Thikë harrimi (Knife of oblivion)
(Prishtinë, 1975); *Trungu ilir* (The
Illyrian stock) (Prishtinë, 1979); *Leja e
njohtimit* (Identity papers) (Prishtinë,
1985); and *Kaosmos* (Chaosmos)
(Prishtinë, 1990). Hamiti now works
for Rilindja Press in Prishtinë.

Blindness

for Jorge Luis Borges

You will die one day, dear Jorge,
One night, all alone and forgotten!
Have you not felt condemned for years now,
For years now to dream in the dark, bereft of your sight?
The Divine Comedy you read with your fingers,
You bathe in the dust of forgotten cities,
Like string you bind feeling and memory in a knot
Compelling the expanses of time to embrace.
You will die one night, dear Jorge,
One day, all alone and forgotten,
At the most you will be a pinch of dust
Borne by the winds to the deserts of Arabia.
Your labyrinth is the invention of solitude
A trap which seizes misery by the throat.
Have you not felt for years now, poor Jorge,
Condemned to dream in the dark?

Sabri Hamiti

The death of young Don Quixote

Literature tells us:
Don Quixote, having read books,
Rushed out of his library
And entered his own life.

His endless adventures
Belong to literature, to the sublime,
Not to life.

Don Quixote has a house full of books
The biggest one in town.
He has a stentorian voice:
He talks all the time, without ever hearing
The truth!

And the books on the shelves
Bite their tongues
And are silent.

Exhausted by their own weight
They break the shelves
And fall onto the head of young Don Quixote,
Burying and suffocating him.

The obituary in the newspaper read:
'He died at his desk.'

George Castrioti*

Every time the frost comes
We recall Your name,
The first and the second,
We do our best to teach it to the children.

Names arise from the shades of the past.
Nish, Kruja, Albulena and Berat.
And again the two names: the first and the second,
One for oneself, one for the others.

Every time the frost comes
We recall Your name.
The living, the suffering. What value has life
When nourished by memories of the past?

The children, who learn names quickly,
Do not want this alone, they want more,
They want life, a name for themselves,
The children who do not grow on memories.

Every time the frost comes
We recall Your name,
When the barking of dogs in the night
Destroys the profound and infinite silence.

A name for oneself and for the others,
Even for mending life
Ask the children when they grow up.
They know no memories, only dreams.

---

* Real name of Scanderbeg (1405–1468), Albanian prince and national hero
who led resistance to the Turks.

Rudolf Marku

(1950—)

Rudolf Marku was born and raised in Lezhë (formerly Alessio). He graduated from the University of Tiranë in 1968 and taught school for some time. Marku worked for a number of years as editor of the Tiranë literary newspaper *Drita* (The light) where he introduced many new and previously ostracized writers to the Albanian public. In the autumn of 1991 he was appointed head of foreign cultural relations at the Albanian Foreign Ministry. Marku's first volume of verse, entitled *Shokët e mi* (My friends) (Tiranë, 1974), led to his banishment to the countryside. It was followed by *Rruga* (The road) (Tiranë, 1977); *Sërishmi* (Once again) (Tiranë, 1982); and *Udhëtim për në vendin e gjërave që njohim* (Voyage to the place of things we know) (Tiranë, 1989).

Rudolf Marku

Caligula's horse

And it came to pass that Caligula's horse
Was proclaimed senator.

A fair horse, almost divine,
It strode majestically into the hall,
Greeted everyone with due regard,
Taking no notice of rank or office, even of the ministers,
And went straight to its appointed place
Modestly,
    As if it were ashamed of being there.

It immediately saw through those around it,
Murderers, profiteers, sycophants, wheelers and dealers
It never assented
    to the conquest of other countries,
To the lowering of salaries, or to the raising of prices,
Nor did it take any notice of pompous speeches,
Never did it applaud,
    but listened to the speeches of the orators
                with sheer indifference
And it never dreamed of taking advantage of its senatorial
Position to publish fat books.

On occasion, glancing at the sleepy faces of its citizens,
It would dream of how it used to frolic in the meadows,
Of the clear blue sky, of spring water.

Later it was engulfed by such sorrow
That the senators began looking askance at it,
They began murmuring about its wild past,
About the dubious company it kept, about its unbridled
                              lifestyle.

Nonetheless, it lived a long life
And it used its power better than anyone else had,
That is:
    not at all!

In memory of my mother

Without a word of warning to anyone
My mother died.

She did not want to bother anyone,
The world had enough problems and worries of its own,
She wandered off, so to speak, on tiptoe.

And since then, I have been more caring of old people,
I give them my seat on the train, on the bus,
Sometimes I feel like taking them into my arms like children.

Even when I don't know them, I talk to them, smile idiotically.
In winter I am afraid they will catch a chill or a cough.
I always avoid the obituaries.

I have no desire to read of her age
Now that I know how to decipher the wrinkles
And to fathom the magic of greying hair.

I have the impression that some day
A letter from afar will fall into my hands
'How are you doing? How are the others?'

Without leaving her address
She continues to wander on tiptoe
Amidst the din of the world, its pain and lamentation.

Arithmetic

One times one
Is not even two.
What number would you get
With me times you?

Visar Zhiti

(1952—)

Visar Zhiti is one of the many talented writers of modern Albania to have suffered appalling persecution for no apparent reason at all. Born on 2 December 1952 in Durrës as the son of a stage actor, he grew up in Lushnjë where he finished school in 1970 and taught in the northern mountain town of Kukës. Zhiti showed an early interest in verse and had published some poems in literary periodicals. In 1973, he was preparing the collection *Rapsodia e jetës së trëndafilave* (Rhapsody of the life of roses) for publication when the purge of intellectuals broke loose at the infamous Fourth Plenary Session of the Party. Zhiti, whose father had earlier come into conflict with the authorities, was selected as one of the numerous
scapegoats in the arts to terrify the intellectual community. The manuscript of the verse collection which he had previously submitted to the editors of the Naim Frashëri Publishing Company was now re-interpreted as containing grave ideological errors and as blackening 'our socialist reality'. There was nothing the poet could say to his interrogators to prove his innocence.

After five years under the people's own Damocles Sword, Visar Zhiti was finally arrested on 10 November 1979 in Kukës, where he was still teaching, and spent the following months in solitary confinement. In order to retain his sanity, he composed and memorized ninety-seven poems (pencil and paper were of course forbidden in jail). Sentenced in April 1980 to ten years in prison for 'agitation and propaganda', Zhiti was transferred to Tiranë prison and from there to the infamous concentration camps from which many talented Albanians never returned: the copper mines of Spaç in Mirdita and the icy mountain camp of Qafë-Bari near Fushë Arrëz. Released on 28 January 1987, he was then permitted to work in a brick factory in his native Lushnjë until the end of the dictatorship. In autumn 1991, Visar Zhiti fulfilled a dream and spent a year working in Italy, and tasting freedom for the first time.

The arrival of Pegasus in my cell

During the day –
Morning, afternoon,
During the night –
Evening, midnight, after midnight
All the mysterious clanking
Reminds me of shackles,
As if the police were coming to take me away,
And fling me into a cavern
    where even fear itself is horror-stricken,
All the clanking . . .
    But what clanking? . . .
        What does it all mean,
        the clanking? . . .
        Petrified, I put my ear
To the loop-hole;
On the small patch of grass – horseshoes.
    A stallion was grazing
As it once did,
As in a dream.
Its handsome body –
Dawn washed by rain and moonlight.
        What good fortune has brought you here?
        Are you not Pegasus?!
I too had verdant dreams,
    as fresh as grass.
Some they trampled,
Others I kept.
Let me throw you some of them –
    eat!
And slowly, with parched lips,
I whispered,
As lovers might have whispered:
'stallion, oh stallion . . .'

It raised its head,
We looked one another in the eye.
I had not seen myself in a mirror for some time,
Had almost forgotten what my face looked like.

I saw myself in the stallion's eyes,
Such human eyes
    shining as if in pain.
I was unkempt,
Bearded and filthy . . .
       and turned away
So as not to startle it with my wild appearance.

(composed in a cell in Kukës prison,
December 1979)

The warbling of moments

How beautifully the nightingale sang
Through the iron bars of my window,
Transforming the very iron
   into the verdant branches of a cherry-tree.

The floor was covered in warbles

And I, on my knees,
Picked them up one by one
Like crumbs of bread,
   like crumbs of life.

(in a prison cell, 1980)

In our cells

They keep us in our cells
For a long time . . .
And when we get out . . .
We lug them with us on our shoulders,
Like a porter
    with a chest of goods.

(1980)

Moments

Moments pass
Over my body
Like lice.

In this prison trench
Filled with the soil of suffering
I sit and wait

How sad it is
To be a warrior
    with no war.

(1982)

Love

How far my night is
                    from your night!
Other nights rise between them like uncrossable mountains.

I sent the road out for you. But it didn't find you.
It grew weary and returned to me.
I sent out the roebuck of my song. But
The hunters shot it and, wounded,
                                it returned to me.
I don't know which direction the wind took. It got lost
In the trees and in the caverns of pain, and returned to me,
                                                blinded.

Rain is falling, robbed of hope.

Tomorrow when day breaks, shall I send out a rainbow
To look for you? Though, as naive as joy itself,
It can only cross one mountain.

I shall set out in the night myself.
I shall search, I shall search, I shall search
Like a hand groping in the darkness of a room,
        to find an extinguished candle.

(Qafë-Bari prison camp, 1983)

The epilogue (of which time makes a preface)

Life is less than hope.

And, still, I write poems
Though no one reads them.
Perhaps the wind does not even read the stars at night,
Maybe the cliffs at the seaside
Feel nothing of the fury of the waves.

And, still, I write poems,
Which have destroyed my life. For seven years
They shrouded my body in barbed wire.
They shred my skin until torrents of life,
　　　　　　like torrents of blood flowed
　　　　　　down to the tips of my toes.
But my soul – not all of my soul,
Only a little bit of it – I was able to extract
From the fissures of my body
　　　　　　and expedite
　　　　　　　　　to love,
　　　　　　　　　　to poetry.

With a little bit of soul I now live on,
Tiny
Like lost bees.

And when you consider
　　　that even inscriptions on gravestones
　　　　　　　　have readers,

You come to realize that poetry is greater than hope.

(Lushnjë, December 1987)

Bloody lips

The open wound
of the gladiator
gurgles out life's end.

The cries of acclamation from the stands
fill the sky with raging tigers.

Waving their arms about, to incite the masses,
The aging notables add an air of dignity to the arena.
Making their separate entries, they k
                              n
                                e
                                  e
                                    l over the still warm corpses
Of the young. Their withered lips they pose
Upon the fresh flowing wounds
And, to prolong their lives – so they believe,
Suck, ravenously suck out the blood, blood, blood.

Fresh blood,
from the sun,
flowing into filthy veins
as if into sewage pipes

And thus the Heart of the Nation is abandoned.

(Lushnjë, 1987)

199

Mimoza Ahmeti

(1963—)

Mimoza Ahmeti from the famed citadel town of Krujë, north of Tiranë, might almost be considered to be part of the second generation of Albanian women writers. She finished her studies of language and literature in Tiranë in 1986 and now teaches literature. Her first volume of verse, entitled *Bëhu i bukur* (Be beautiful) (Tiranë, 1986), was well received by critics. It was followed by *Sidomos nesër* (Especially tomorrow) (Tiranë, 1989), a collection of fifty-nine poems on intensely personal, though at the same time universal themes, which have proved her to be a virtuoso of poetic technique.

Mimoza Ahmeti

Song

Were you to rise
Not like a flower
But like a volcano,

Were you to soar
Not like a bird
But like the sun,

Were you to fall
Not like a leaf
But like lightning,

Let me be
The flower, the bird and the leaf.

Rhetorical question for Comrade X

You know well how to disguise
The pallor of your cheeks with rouge,
But how do you intend to disguise
The pallor of your soul?

Paper

I do not want you to write about your separation,
Separation is not worthy of your muse
For your verse exchanges signals
Even with the coldest, the most distant star.

A white piece of paper, completely white,
With a blue smudge, a blue smudge in the corner
Is the verse you should devote
To her departure . . .

It would be awful

It would be awful
Waking up the same every morning.

But it would be even worse
Seeing the end of the day
With morning eyes.

Outside and inside me

Outside me
The whole world reels in battle and dream.

But inside me too
Its voice resounds.

Outside me
They are loving, killing, giving birth
To millions.

But inside me too
Love
Murder
Birth
Are just as active.

Extinction

You were once blue-coloured. You have grown dark.
Do you not know what this means?
Remember how my ray
Shot into your sky like an arrow.
                              – Remember.
The satisfaction of security has darkened you.
Now with your hands in your pockets you make fun of the
                                                    others,
But why does your face
No longer bear that lordly smile of tranquillity?

As a warning on those April evenings
You interrupted my every word with a leaden silence.
Blue-coloured, you blue egoist,
Slowly you went out in my hands.

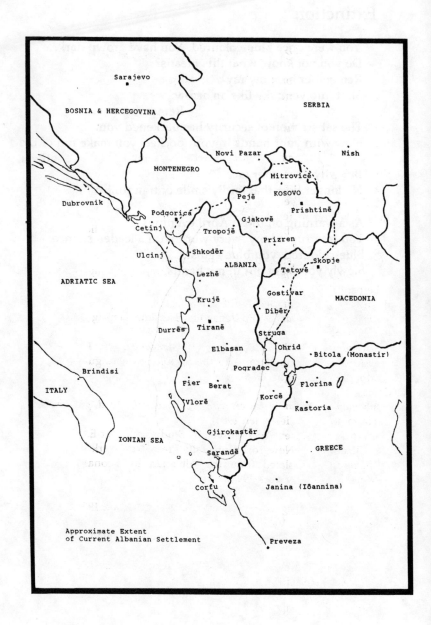

Selected Bibliography

on the Albanian language
and modern Albanian verse

Anthologie de la poésie albanaise. (8 Nëntori, Tiranë 1983)

BIHIKU, Koço
History of Albanian literature. (8 Nëntori, Tiranë 1980).

BIHIKU, Koço (ed.)
Historia e letërsisë shqiptare të realizmit socialist. (Akademia e Shkencave, Tiranë 1978).

BLAND, William B. (ed.)
Albania. World Bibliographical Series, vol. 94. (Clio Press, Oxford 1988).

BUCHHOLZ, Oda, FIEDLER, Wilfried & UHLISCH, Gerda
Wörterbuch Albanisch Deutsch. (VEB Verlag Enzyklopädie, Leipzig 1977).

BUCHHOLZ, Oda & FIEDLER, Wilfried
Albanische Grammatik. (VEB Verlag Enzyklopädie, Leipzig 1987).

BYRON, Janet
Selection among alternates in language standardization. The case of Albanian (Contributions to the Sociology of Language 12). (Mouton, The Hague 1976).

CAMAJ, Martin
Albanian grammar with exercises, chrestomathy and glossary. (Harrassowitz, Wiesbaden 1984).
Selected poetry. New York University Studies on Near East Civilization 14. (New York University Press, New York 1990).
Palimpsest. Translated from the Albanian by Leonard Fox. (Munich and New York 1991).

DANIEL, Odile
Albanie. Une bibliographie historique. (CNRS, Paris, ca. 1987).

DESNICKAJA, Agnija Vasil'evna
Albanskaja literatura i albanskij jazyk. (Nauka, Leningrad 1987).

DRIZARI, Nelo
Albanian literature. in: *Dictionary of Modern European Literature* (ed. SMITH, Horatio) (OUP, London 1948).
Albanian–English and English–Albanian dictionary. Enlarged edition. (Ungar, New York 1957).

DURAKU, Nebil
Shkrimtarët e Kosovës '43–'83. (Rilindja, Prishtinë 1984).

209

Bibliography

DURO, Ilo & HYSA, Ramazan
Albanian-English dictionary. Fjalor shqip–anglisht. (Tiranë 1981, Prishtinë 1988).

ELSIE, Robert
Dictionary of Albanian literature. (Greenwood, Westport & New York 1986).
Einem Adler gleich. Anthologie albanischer Lyrik vom 16. Jahrhundert bis zur Gegenwart. Herausgegeben und aus dem Albanischen von Robert Elsie. (Olms, Hildesheim Zürich & New York 1988).
Modern Albanian literature. in: *Albanien in Umbruch.* Eine Bestandsaufnahme. Untersuchungen zur Gegenswartskunde Südosteuropas. Herausgegeben vom Südost-Institut. Schriftleitung Franz-Lothar Altmann. Band 28 (Munich 1990).
Albanian literature in Greek script. The eighteenth- and early nineteenth-century Orthodox tradition in Albanian writing. in: *Byzantine and Modern Greek Studies,* Birmingham, 15 (1991).
Albanische Literatur und Kultur nach sechsundvierzig Jahren Sozialismus. Ein Zustandsbericht. in: *Südosteuropa.* Zeitschrift für Gegenwartsforschung, Munich, 11–12 (1991).
Evolution and revolution in modern Albanian literature. in: *World Literature Today.* Literary quarterly of the University of Oklahoma. Vol. 65.2 (Spring) 1991.
Rezeption albanischer Literatur im deutschen Sprachraum. in: *Aspekte der Albanologie.* Akten des Kongresses 'Stand und Aufgaben der Albanologie heute' 3.–5. Oktober 1988, Universität zu Köln. Herausgegeben von Walter Breu, Rolf Ködderitzsch und Hans-Jürgen Sasse. Balkanologische Veröffentlichungen Band 18 (Harrassowitz, Wiesbaden 1991).
The Scutarine Catholic contribution to the development of nineteenth-century Albanian literature. in: *Albanian Catholic Bulletin,* San Francisco, Vol. XII (1991).
Albanian literature in English translation: a short survey. in: *The Slavonic and East European Review,* London, 70.2 (April 1992).
Fjalor anglisht-shqip për shkolla të mesme. (Enti e teksteve, Prishtinë 1972).
Fjalori anglisht-shqip. (Ministria e arësimit, Tiranë 1966).

GJERQEKU, Enver, KELMENDI, Ramiz & MEKULI, Hasan
Panoramë e letërsisë bashkëkohore shqipe në Jugosllavi. (Enti për Botimin e Teksteve i RS të Sërbisë, Belgrade 1964).

GRULICH, Rudolf
Regen in einer Legende. Albanische Lyrik vom Amselfeld. (Heiligenhof 1977).

HETZER, Armin & FINGER, Zuzana
Lehrbuch der vereinheitlichten albanischen Schriftsprache. 3.
vollständig überarbeitete Auflage mit Übungen und Lösungen.
(Helmut Buske, Hamburg 1989).

HETZER, Armin & ROMAN, Viorel S. (ed.)
Albanien, ein bibliographischer Forschungsbericht mit Titelübersetzungen und Standortnachweisen. Albania, a bibliographical research survey with location codes. (Saur, Munich 1983).

ISMAJLI, Rexhep (ed.)
Rrënjë e fortë. Poezia arbëreshe e ditëve tona. (Rilindja, Prishtinë 1978)
Poezia e sotme arbëreshe. (Rilindja, Prishtinë 1990).

JORGAQI, Nasho & SINANI, Hysen (ed.)
Degë e blertë. Antologji e poezisë së sotme arbëreshe. (Naim Frashëri, Tiranë 1980).

KACORI, Thoma
A handbook of Albanian. (Sofia University, Sofia 1979).

KADARE, Ismail
Poèmes 1958–1988. Préface de Alain Bosquet. (Fayard, Paris 1989).

KIÇI, Gasper
Albanian–English dictionary. Fjalor shqip-anglisht. (Rome 1978).

KIÇI, Gasper & ALIKO, Hysni
English–Albanian dictionary. Fjalor anglisht-shqip. (Rome 1969).

KOLIQI, Ernesto
Antologia della lirica albanese. (All' Insegna del Pesce d'Oro, Milan 1963).
Saggi di letteratura albanese. Studi e testi 5. (Olschki, Florence 1972).

Les Lettres albanaises. Revue trimestrielle littéraire et artistique publiée par l'Union des Ecrivains et Artistes d'Albanie. (Tiranë 1978–).

LUSSU, Joyce
La poesia degli albanesi. (ERI, Turin 1977).

MALAMAS, Lambros
Anafora stên albanikê logotekhnia 1500–1986. (Eleuthero Pneuma, Iôannina 1987).

MANN, Stuart E.
Albanian literature. An outline of prose, poetry and drama. (Quaritch, London 1955).

MANNING, Clarence
Albanian poetry. in: *Princeton Encyclopedia of Poetry and Poetics.* Ed. Preminger, Warnke & Harrison. (Princeton UP, Princeton 1965).

METAIS, Michel
Ismaïl Kadaré et la nouvelle poésie albanaise. (Oswald, Paris 1973).

211

Bibliography

MIGJENI
Migjeni. Freie Verse. Gedichte aus Albanien. Übertragen von Robert Elsie. (Schulz-Kirchner, Idstein 1987).
Free verse. Translated from Albanian by Robert Elsie. (8 Nëntori Publishing House, Tiranë 1991).

NËNTORI (NËNDORI)
E përmuajshme letrare artistike shoqërore politike. Organi i Lidhjes së Shkrimtarëve dhe Artistëve të Shqipërisë. (Tirane 1954–).

NEWMARK, Leonard, HAZNEDARI, Ismail, HUBBARD, Philip & PRIFTI, Peter
Spoken Albanian. (Spoken Language Services, Ithaca 1980).

NEWMARK, Leonard, HUBBARD, Philip & PRIFTI, Peter
Standard Albanian: a reference grammar for students. (Stanford University Press, Stanford, 1982).

PETROTTA, Gaetano
Popolo, lingua e letteratura albanese. 2a tiratura con aggiunte e correzioni. (Pontificia, Palermo 1932).
Svoglimento storico della cultura e della letteratura albanese. (Boccone del Povero, Palermo 1950).

PIPA, Arshi
Panorama of contemporary Albanian literature. in: *Zeitschrift für Balkanologie,* Berlin, 7 (1969/70).
Modern and contemporary Albanian poetry. in: *Books abroad,* Norman Oklahoma, 44.1 (winter 1970).
Albanian literature, social perspectives. Trilogia Albanica 3. Albanische Forschungen 19. (Trofenik, Munich 1978).
The politics of language in Socialist Albania. (Columbia UP, New York 1989).
Contemporary Albanian literature. East European Monographs 305. (Columbia University Press, New York 1991).

PIPA, Arshi & REPISHTI, Sami (ed.)
Studies on Kosova. East European Monographs 155. (Boulder 1984).

PODRIMJA, Ali
Ich sattle das Ross den Tod. (Weiser, Klagenfurt 1991).

PODRIMJA, Ali & HAMITI, Sabri (ed.)
The sad branch. Albanian poetry in Yugoslavia. Dega e pikëlluar. Poezi shqipe në Jugosllavi. (Rilindja, Prishtinë 1984).

POGONI, Bardhyl
Contemporary Albanian poems. Translations and comments by Bardhyl Pogoni. (Dragotti, Naples 1985).

QOSJA, Rexhep
Antologjia e lirikës shqipe. Botim i dytë i plotësuar dhe i përmirësuar. (Enti i teksteve, Prishtinë 1979).

QVICK, Ullmar
Örnarna och bergen. Albansk poesi. (Rallarros, Gävle 1979).

RESSULI, Namik
Albanian literature. (Vatra, Boston 1987).
Roads lead only one way. A survey of modern poetry from Kosova.
The Kosova Association of Literary Translators. (Rilindja,
Prishtinë 1988).
SCHIRO, Giuseppe [junior]
Storia della letteratura albanese. (Nuova Accademia Editrice,
Milan 1959)
Shêjzat. Le Plèiadi. E përkohshme kulturore, shoqnore e artistike.
Revista culturale, sociale ed artistica. Founder and proprietor:
Ernesto Koliqi. Editor: Martin Camaj. (Rome 1957–1974).
SHEMA, Isak & RUGOVA, Ibrahim
Bibliografi e kritikës letrare shqiptare 1944–1974. (Instituti Albano-
logjik, Prishtinë 1976).
SHKRELI, Azem
The call of the owl. Translated from the Albanian by John
Hodgson. (Kosova Association of Literary Translators, Prishtinë
1989).
SHUTERIQI, Dhimitër (ed.)
*Historia e letërsisë shqiptare që nga fillimet deri te lufta antifashiste
nacionalçlirimtare.* (Akademia e Shkencave, Tiranë 1983; Rilindja,
Prishtinë 1990).
SHUTERIQI, Dhimitër, BIHIKU, Koço & DOMI, Mahir (ed.)
Historia e letërsisë shqipe 1–2. (Tiranë 1959, 1960; Prishtinë 1975).
SOLANO, Francesco
Manuale di lingua albanese. Elementi di morfologia e sintassi,
esercizi, cenni sui dialetti. (Biondi, Cosenza 1988).
STEFANLLARI, Ilo
Fjalor anglisht-shqip. (Rilindja, Prishtinë 1988).
TOMA, Ana, KARAPICI, Zana & RADOVICKA, *Lumnije*
Gjuhe letrare shqipe. Libër mësimi 1–2. (Libri shkollor, Tiranë
1989).
VINCA, Agim
Struktura e zhvillimit të poezisë së sotme shqipe (1945–1980).
(Rilindja, Prishtinë 1985).
Orët e poezisë. (Rilindja, Prishtinë 1990).
Zieh dich zurück in den Vers Homers. Moderne Dichtung aus
Kosovo. (Verband der Literarischen Übersetzer Kosovos, Mitro-
vicë e Titos 1990).
Zjarri. Il fuoco. Rivista di cultura albanese. (San Demetrio Corone
1968–)
ZOTOS, Alexandre
La poésie albanaise. Les cahiers de poésie-rencontres 26. (Lyons
1989).
ZYMBERI, Isa
Colloquial Albanian. (Routledge, London 1991).